PRACTICAL HOT RODDER'S GUIDE

JB

D0898956

First Published in 1997 by
Graffiti Publications Pty. Ltd.
P.O. Box 232, Castlemaine,
Victoria 3450, Australia.
Phone 61 3 54723653,
Fax 61 3 54723805.

Graffiti Publications books are also available at discounts in bulk quantity for industrial or sales promotional use. For details write to Graffiti Publications Pty. Ltd., P.O. Box 232, Castlemaine 3450, Victoria, Australia.

Front cover: Street rodders are individuals and so are their vehicles. The only rules when building a street rod are to satisfy the desires of the owner, but most street rods still fall into a styling category. Our cover shows a collection of street rods of various styles ranging from high tech, extensively restyled vehicles through to period replicas of past times – the nostalgia rods.

ISBN 0 949398 49 7

Printed and bound in Australia.

CONTENTS

INTRODUCTION

Good information; every street rodder yearns for it when building his own project car and yet every rodder is an individual who likes his vehicle to project his own personality. But street rodders are also ingenious people. They can take someone else's ideas, or part of them, and adapt them to their own use in such a way that the end result appears to be another new idea. That's what this book is about, good ideas that can be adapted to your own project or that can sow the seed of a totally new custom touch.

In gathering the information used in this book I have travelled widely and tried to gain material from a broad cross section of the rodding move-

ment. Mixed with some more in-depth technical articles this wealth of information and photos will hopefully become a source book for ideas that you will refer to again and again as you build your own street rod.

I've learnt a lot from books myself in twenty-five years of hands-on involvement in this great hobby. There is no substitute for experience when it comes to building your own hot rod though, so I hope that this book will serve as an inspiration for your own project and you will, as a result, get out into your own garage and make it come true.

Larry O'Toole

LOOK AND LEARN

The easiest way to learn new tricks is to check what other rodders have done in similar situations, then adapt those ideas, mixed with some of your own ingenuity, to suit your own car. The major street rod events provide great opportunities for absorbing new ideas and making comparisons.

One of the most fascinating aspects of this great hobby is the inexhaustible ability of street rodders to come up with new ideas. Ever since those rebellious hot rodders of the thirties and forties started stripping down and modifying their cars for better performance they have looked for ways to refine the process. The fifties and sixties saw the hobby move laterally to incorporate show cars, customs and drag racing but still the essence was the same; find a way to do it better or make it go faster. Now in the nineties all those elements are still the essential ingredients that constitute the modern street rod or custom.

True, the emphasis in some areas has changed. Whereas the early rodders were basically concerned with one factor, increased performance, the modern rodder tends to treat his car as an overall expression of his or her own individuality. That's not to say performance isn't still important but these days the hobby has a much broader perspective. There are still those who build hot rods with

acceleration and speed, or at least the image of such performance, as their basic criteria. For others the emphasis is on style and cleanliness while some yearn for nostalgia with the extra performance that makes their particular street rod a joy to drive often, if not every day.

It doesn't really matter what style your ideal street rod takes, either in your own mind or in cold hard parts on your garage floor. Trends come and go as this great hobby continues to evolve and continue to evolve it will for many, many years. Every rodder has a part to play in that evolution whether by adapting someone else's ideas or contributing their own; perhaps even a combination of the two.

Unfortunately not all new ideas are good ideas, so you need to be alert to factors that influence the suitability of certain modifications. This can become a very broad subject as those factors could be as diverse as differing legal requirements from state to state and country to country, through to

5

Using a severely dropped axle like the one shown here will get your rod riding in the weeds but take care, if a tire suddenly deflates the axle will come into contact with the road surface before the wheel rim. The result could be disastrous, especially if travelling at highway speeds.

practicality and safety. Let me give you just a couple of examples.

It is currently fairly popular to remove external door handles and fit electric solenoid operated mechanisms in doors. Makes for a smooth looking body on the outside but this is a modification that in some places is illegal, requiring some external mechanical method of opening the door. Of course that just prompts the thinking rodder to come up with an alternative that overcomes the situation. You will find examples of such solutions right here in this book.

When it comes to practical safety you need to really pay attention. Sometimes that really zoomy looking street rod you admire so much could in fact be a death trap. Look closely before you incorporate an idea that may be unsafe. More examples include severely dropped front axles that really get the car down low but often mean that a suddenly deflating front tire allows the axle or its associated components to come into contact with the road before the wheel rim does. No fun at highway speeds!

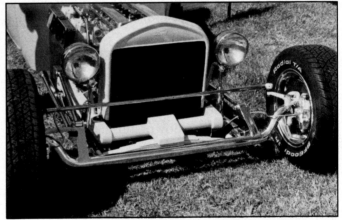

Suicide suspension could be just that if you don't incorporate some form of restraining device to prevent the chassis from dropping onto the roadway in the event of a broken front spring or shackle.

Suicide front ends on fad cars are another. The name is very apt. Without some form of safety override a broken spring or shackle on such a front end could mean disaster. Yet the solution is as simple as a cleverly designed license plate bracket that contacts the axle in the event of such a failure

Next time you visit a car show or rod run take the time to evaluate your own ideas compared to a similar style of street rod. Take photos or notes too if necessary, even talk to the owner. Often this will reveal that the reason for doing something a certain way is dictated by factors that you hadn't taken into account.

The solution to the suicide front end problem shown on the previous page could be as simple as cleverly designed license plate mounting bracket like that shown here. If the spring or a shackle fails the front of the chassis can only drop until the bracket contacts the axle.

and prevents the frame from dropping to the road surface.

The operative phrase that sums up this introductory chapter is the heading itself. Look and learn. Don't just accept that someone else's idea is the best or only way a given problem can be

solved. Teach yourself to analyse every situation and solve its problems, if you recognise any, before you then apply it to your own vehicle. Who knows, your solution to someone else's mistake could become the next hot idea!

Next time you visit a car show or rod run take the time to evaluate your own ideas compared to a similar style of street rod. Take photos or notes too if necessary, even talk to the owner. Often this will reveal that the reason for doing something a certain way is dictated by factors that you hadn't taken into account. Another great way to formulate ideas and put them into practise is to spend a day in a wrecking yard. Here you will find a host of good ideas incorporated into factory produced vehicles that you can borrow or adapt to suit your own needs. The basic criteria though is still the same. Look and learn before you jump right into your own particular project. The end result will speak for itself.

Front end styling doesn't get much smoother and neater than this '47 Ford example owned by J.T. and Carol Winfrey. Headlights have been frenched and accessory indicators set into the fender below the headlights for a fully integrated appearance. Fully painted finish is state of the art.

The options open to any hot rodder when deciding on a style for his or her hot rod are many and varied. In the end you're the only person you have to please though, so don't be drawn into giving your car the sort of treatment that you don't particularly like just because it's trendy. Remember you'll most likely want to keep this car for a while so make sure it is the style that you want.

Once you have settled on a style you can then start planning out each part of the car. Of course having decided on a particular style remember it is important to carry it right through the car. No use going with a bumperless, high-tech style at the front if the rear end is pure resto-rod! The same applies to the interior and even the engine bay. A hot rod that is 'in tune' from front to back, inside and out, is a hot rod that commands attention because it has "got it all together". Not only will it command attention, you will also be much happier with the end result because the car will look balanced in all departments.

Where to start? This chapter is about front end styling so we will only concern ourselves with that portion for the moment. Remember though, to first decide what style the whole car will be and design your front end treatment accordingly. If bumpered and full fendered is the way for you to go then you will need to first make sure you have all the parts necessary and that they are in good condition or at least salvageable. Now it's time to make all the little changes you have planned in order to achieve the result you want. Should you be opting for a totally stock appearance then there isn't much to do apart from make sure you have everything you need and more importantly that the parts all fit together properly. No use getting the spray gun out yet if you haven't trial fitted everything in mock-up form.

Okay, so in most cases hot rods don't stay purely with the original factory design. Little individual touches to an otherwise fairly standard front end design can make a world of difference. For instance on a fat fendered rod it may only be something as simple as making new bumper irons so that they mount under the fender instead of passing through the lower edge. Fill in the old recesses and maybe even shorten the irons a little to draw the bumper in closer to the body and all of a sudden your rod takes on a totally different appearance.

Let's look at another example, this time a fenderless hiboy style car. In this case all your front suspension is going to be exposed so you will want it to look as attractive and well balanced as you can. Independent front suspension is popular on hot rods these days but if you want a traditional looking hiboy it will usually look out of place on such a car. While the traditional beam axle and radius rods or four bar might not ride quite as nice as a fully independent front end, your hiboy will generally look far better with the early Ford based front end.

It doesn't just stop there though. Even such simple things as wheel and tire choice will make an enormous difference to a hiboy or open wheel style car so take the time to make sure you get it right. You'll be far happier in the long run, even if it does take a little longer and cost a little more to get the style you really want.

While we're talking open wheel cars let's go one step further. In some states and countries it isn't legal to run without fenders. Often the solution is to fit cycle fenders to comply with the law for driving purposes, even if sometimes they 'fall off' for a show or static display. But so often these cycle fenders are just an afterthought and when bolted in place, which they will be most of the time, they really detract from the car. Even if you always display your hiboy without the fenders it's

There are some neat tricks here even though the hiboy is really too low to be practical for normal street use. Extreme lowness is gained by using quarter elliptic springs running parallel to the inside of the chassis rail. The springs act as the lower locater so only a top 'four bar' is needed on the outside.

worth taking extra care to make them look as if they belong with the car. You'll feel better about the car if you make them fit properly even if you paint them matt black so that they 'blend in' with the tires.

Now let's turn our attention to grilles. Here's another part of the average hot rod front end that is often treated as an afterthought. Why not plan to make your grille 'belong' to the front end. There are a number of ways of achieving this and again it will have a lot to do with the styling of your car.

ment only makes such 'uglies' stand out more. The solution may be as simple as adding a little flatting base to the paint so that these items reflect less light and consequently don't attract the viewers eye so readily, or it may be that you are better off to use matt, or satin black on such items to help them 'disappear' behind the grille. Whichever way you go, don't be afraid to change it if it doesn't look right the first time. Remember it's only paint!

Enough of the pontificating from me. The main idea of this book is to bring you a wide selection

The front of Tony Kuchel's '37 Ford coupe has been given the all-paint treatment and cleaned of all interruptions to the smooth flowing lines. Notice how the stock bumper iron openings in the fenders have been filled and new irons located under the lower edge of the fender. The front license plate bolts to the right side iron as well. It would be a simple operation to completely remove the bumper to give the front end a different look again.

If you have elected to go with the all-paint look, so popular in these days, you will need to make sure your grille is very straight and that it fits properly. Often rodders will paint the radiator and front mounted fans, oil coolers, etc., so that they match the paintwork of the grille. Think about this one carefully because often such treat-

of examples of how others have treated the styling of their rods. By presenting them to you in this format we hope you take the opportunity, not to copy so much as to absorb their ideas and blend them into your own. Let's go front end viewing in pictorial form.

This Model A roadster pickup sits very low and uses independent front end for a smoother ride. Sometimes it can be hard to achieve this in a Model A because the amount of room under the fender is quite restricted for height. Fred Kooistra has overcome the problem by recessing the suspension into the fender with a smoothed in bulge added to accommodate the suspension tower. By smoothing and blending the fender bulge it is hardly noticed when finish painted and partly hidden by a stock Model A headlight on a dropped headlight bar.

Ray Langford's '48 Ford coupe has many styling improvements incorporated into the front. The headlights have been frenched into the fender and now fit in place from behind. All the grille parts have been painted instead of chrome plated and there is a new lower grille panel added in place of the original full width bumper. It all adds up to a very clean styling exercise that works.

11

Neat nerf bar arrangement on Charlie Seaberg's '34 Ford coupe does duty as a grille protector and front license plate mount and also provides a home for the front turn signals which appear to have come from a motorcycle. The nerf bar mounts to the original bumper holes in the front of the chassis and could easily be replaced with a stock bumper if required.

The headlights on Ian Hickey's '35 Ford coupe are aftermarket Dietz items fitted with halogen beams and are mounted in the original position. Note how the lights are mounted right down on the base as the original, larger units were to give an improved "standard" appearance. Also check out the front bumper irons which have been reshaped to pull the stock bumper closer to the bodywork for a tidier appearance.

You can't get the front of a fat fendered car much cleaner than this! The grille of this '35 Ford has been changed to a two piece construction with outer shell and an insert that fits from behind. The lower edge has been changed in the process to give it a finished edge rather than the wrapped under style of the original. Eliminating the bumper and filling the bumper iron cut-outs adds to the smooth look as does the switch to smaller King Bee headlights. No chrome plating is used anywhere on the front of this Ford.

Model A Fords tend to respond well to dropped headlight bars even when teamed with the stock large diameter headlights. Halogen inserts behind the original lenses guarantee that night time vision will be greatly enhanced. Look carefully and you will also notice the small turn signals hidden under the headlights as well. This car uses an independent front end with front mounted rack and pinion steering and the owner has cleverly reshaped the front splash apron to cover the steering but at the same time maintain an original style. It also provides a handy mounting point for the front license plate.

Here's another '35 Ford on which the owner, Bob Scott has done away with the stock bumper openings in the lower fender area but this one uses short alloy nerf bars to provide some frontal protection. Again the front including the grille has been treated to the all paint look but notice how Dietz headlights have been slightly sunken into the fenders forward of and lower than the original '35 location to give the car a lower profile.

Rod Henderson owns this Model A tudor that uses an independent Holden front end complete with stabiliser bar. The forward projection of the Holden crossmember means the original splash apron won't fit any more so Rod made up this gently curved but shallower than stock version to hide the front end and keep the front styling all in context. Again stock headlights with sealed beams hidden behind stock lenses are used on a dropped headlight bar.

Another view of the really low '32 Ford hiboy roadster shown at the start of this chapter reveals a neat angled front shock absorber mount and accessory headlight mounted to the side of the grille shell. While a roadster that sits this low looks really cool it would certainly suffer lower grille damage if subjected to normal road use. It will also be the first thing to come in contact with the road surface in the event of a blowout! Horizontal bars in the grille insert accentuate the low profile even further.

Stock front bumper and headlights are retained on this '36 Ford coupe but the rest of the front end styling is typical modern street rod. All the bright trim has been left off the grille and hood hinge, the decorative V8 bullnose ornament has been replaced with a smooth painted version and even the triple side bars have been removed from the hood sides. The grille has been painted to match the bodywork but there are a couple of other neat tricks on the front of this '36 as well. Look carefully and you will see that the normally separate panels either side of the grille have been blended into the front fenders and the stock horn grilles have been removed and filled. The front is less cluttered looking, yet there is still no doubt this is a '36 Ford.

15

This one could have you guessing at its true identity due to the extent of remodelling done to the front sheetmetal. It is in fact a '39 Ford standard tudor owned by Steve and Deb Huntington of Algonquin, Illinois. All brightwork has been removed from the grille and front sheetmetal, the headlights have been frenched into the fenders and the normally partially vented hood sides filled for a smoother appearance. Lack of bumper and hood ornament makes it clean, clean, clean.

Tilt fronts have been around for a number of years but they often don't look right because they can be difficult to align, especially when the front fender is divided as on this chopped '48 Chev pickup. Bill Strohl overcame that problem on his pickup by incorporating three aligning dowels in the joining faces of the fenders to ensure the front locates properly and can't move around too much as the vehicle is being driven. Did you notice the neat tunnelled radio antenna just in front of the windshield pillar?

Now here is some slick styling on a '37 Ford "phaeton" owned by Eric and Kaye Salcy. Apart from the extremely low stance check out the extra "style line" in the front fender, increased slant in the windshield and sunshade formed into the front of the roof. From there forward it's all smooth, all painted and almost too good to be true. Keep looking and you will see countless other subtle changes have been made to this truly beautiful street rod.

You may have to look twice to recognise that Ed and Linda Post's street rod is actually a '38 Chevy tudor. The one piece tilting grille and hood give it a totally different appearance as do the fender mounted and blended in headlights. Late model gas rams hold the front in the up position for easy access to the engine bay while small diameter rubber tube acts as cowl lacing to prevent the painted surfaces from coming into contact when the hood is lowered.

While the all-paint look is certainly popular this photo shows that a blend of paint and some original brightwork can be tasteful, too. Butch Straw's '38 Plymouth sedan has painted grille and headlights but retains the chrome plated original bumper bar with over riders for a highlight and a touch of originality. Colour coded headlight covers are a neat idea.

Even the non-Fords respond well to some cleaning up and smoothing off. This one is a '33 Plymouth coupe owned by Robert Hannan. Removing the front bumper and cleaning up the leading edges of the fenders has greatly improved the frontal appearance. The popular all paint look has been used and turn signals have been cleverly incorporated into the leading edges of the fenders. With all the bright trimwork gone there is nothing to take your attention away from the fact that this is one clean Mopar!

There are scores of custom touches on Wayne Medlin's Model A coupe from Boulder, Colorado. At the front we find completely moulded front rail covers and turn signals neatly moulded into the bottom of the grille shell. The clean appearance of the front end is enhanced by the lack of headlight bar, made possible by mounting the headlights to the sides of the grille shell. There is barely an exposed nut or bolt to be seen anywhere on this car.

There's obviously something different about the front of this '32 Ford tudor but you may have to study it for a while to pick the changes. Look at the lower front edge of the fenders and you will see that they have been reshaped with more definition where they meet the frame horns. The splash apron also features a sharper design in keeping with the fenders. Now turn your attention to the dropped headlight bar and you will see that it no longer bolts to the fender but rather passes through it. Only subtle changes but they make this '32 stand apart from all the rest.

Perfect sheetmetal and superb attention to detail make this Model A roadster pickup nothing short of outstanding. The grille shell is filled and fitted with polished aluminum bars, the fuel tank filler has been eliminated from the cowl and there's not a ripple to be seen anywhere. Mounting the headlights on short bars that connect to the grille shell and eliminating the front bumper means there is nothing to interrupt your view of this black masterpiece either.

A custom front bumper like this ribbed Briz version can change the appearance of your '34 Ford. This one is further enhanced by the use of milled aluminum mounting brackets and it has been painted to match the body colour of the car. Examine the joining area of the front fenders under the grille and you will see that the original style joining bracket has been eliminated as well and the fenders fitted flush to each other.

Stuart Woodman chose a '40 Chevy pickup for his street rod and treated the front end to some neat alterations. The custom made grille features repro '32 Ford grille bars and it is painted to match the body. Small oval shaped front turn signals are from a late model Japanese car but echo the shape of the popular '39 Ford teardrop tail lights which have been around street rodding for years. Take a look at the smooth front bumper that has attaching bolts welded to the rear side to allow the front face of the bumper to be one completely smooth chrome plated surface.

There are many neat custom touches on the front of John Dyer's '32 Ford hiboy roadster. The frame boxing inside the front frame horns was milled with grooves before being welded in place and the same milled features continue up the headlight/shock absorber mounts. John's show display also gives us the opportunity to check out the tidy disc brake rotor covers and spin-on type lug covers. Once again we spy some neat little front turn signals.

21

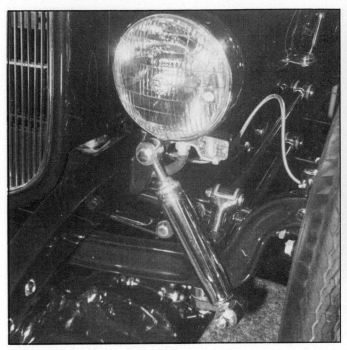

Nothing too extraordinary about the front end of Peter Quaife's '32 Ford until you look closely at the lower headlight region. See the neat little turn signal mounted on its own stepped aluminum bracket that makes the indicator appear as if it truly belongs to the car.

A different appearance for the front of Tony and Sue Correa's '37 Chevy has been achieved by using strips of polished aluminum as grille bars within the otherwise original opening. An early style tie bar acts as a nerf bar out front and provides protection for the custom grille.

Robert Wilson's chopped '35 Ford coupe sits very low thanks to some clever work that you can't readily see. The body has been channelled over the chassis but the car remains fully fendered so you can't immediately pick that it has been channelled. The all paint look extends from grille right through to the rear end and includes the smooth style running boards. Color coded headlight covers and painted windshield frame ensure the clean paint look is complete and lack of bumpers make it appear shorter and lower than would otherwise be the case.

It's not hard to find items of interest on Neil and Margaret Baker's '33 Ford roadster, the whole car is virtually custom built from front to back. The roadster uses a complete custom tube type frame and the fibreglass bodywork attaches to it somewhat like a race car. The whole front section lifts off in one piece to reveal blown big block Chevy power and coil-over suspension on a dropped tube axle. Close inspection reveals trick headlight mounts that incorporate the front turn signals and shock absorber mounts. Focus your attention on the upper front tube of the frame and you will also see that it does double duty as the expansion tank for the radiator. Small, neat rubber mounts insulate the radiator from the frame.

Hardly a single part of this fat fendered Ford has escaped the custom touch. Study this photo carefully and you will soon absorb at least a few of the changes. The forward opening hood and custom grille are readily noticed but also check how a late model bumper has been blended into the lower grille panel. The smooth one-piece windshield gives the car a more modern appearance as does the "crown" style painted roof bar that divides the otherwise fabric roof. Keep looking, there's plenty more!

Usually the joint between the front fenders on a '33-'34 Ford has a special bracket to tie the two together. Often fiberglass fenders do away with this bracket for a cleaner appearance as has been done on Russell Wright's '34 Vicky phaeton. Russell has gone one step further here though by using custom paint to highlight the feature. Look in the mirror under the grille and you can see how a return has been included on the underside of the fenders to allow them to be bolted firmly together.

The clean, smooth styling of a lot of modern street rods can leave the grille area vulnerable to damage on the road so some form of protection is often called for. On this '35 Ford coupe a pair of neat nerf bars joined with a vee shaped tie bar perform that function. King Bee type headlights improve the lighting situation and also notice how small turn signals have been semi-tunnelled into the fenders under the headlight stands.

Sometimes a more masculine approach to providing some frontal protection for your precious early fenders works, too. Check out this phantom '34 Ford roadster pickup which uses a large diameter chrome tube nerf bar. The same styling treatment has been used at the rear end for an integrated result. The headlights demand some attention as well being mounted close to the fender rather than on stock staunchions which can give the front of a clean car like this a gooseneck appearance. The painted grille is a fiberglass repro surround with custom made steel insert that overcomes the need to locate and repair an expensive original item.

25

Phil Air has put together a unique and very high quality Model A pickup by doing all the work himself and using readily available and inexpensive running gear. The front styling has been cleaned up as well by moulding the fuel tank into the cowl and fitting a custom made front splash apron that conforms to the lower edge of the chassis rails. It covers a Holden independent front end, a long time favorite of Australian street rodders. Stock Model A headlights on a dropped headlight bar retain their polished finish but the grille shell has been painted to match the body-work.

Making your own custom bumper irons as Greg Jones has done on his '37 Ford coupe has a couple of advantages. The bumper can be pulled in closer to the body for a more refined appearance as is common on modern contemporary street rods. At the same time shaping the brackets to suit a new location so that they pass under the botom edge of the fender rather than through it leaves the front of the fender nice and smooth looking. Should you desire a slight change of style you could now leave the bumper off altogether and the front end styling still looks nice and clean. Note the neat little turn signal set into the leading edge of the fender.

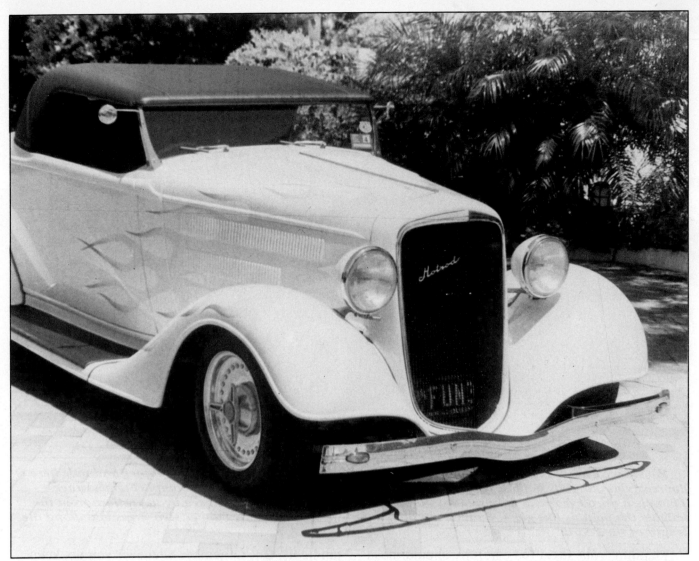

At first glance the front end styling on this '34 Chevrolet roadster may appear to be fairly standard. Look again and you will notice that it uses a '35 Ford bumper and it suits the car perfectly. Late model side turn signal units have been mounted on the bumper and their oval design fits in nicely with the early street rod styling. To further enhance the styling of his Chevy the owner Graham Cowan also reshaped the leading edge of the front fenders to make them flow better in the lower area where they echo the shape of the bottom of the grille. Headlights may appear stock too, but in fact they use quartz halogen inserts from a motorcycle that are almost a perfect fit in the original Chevy headlight buckets.

We showed you this superb Model A roadster pickup in the front end styling chapter and now here is the rear view. Slightly bobbed fenders and shortened bed give the car a more compact appearance. There is a third eye brake light set into the back of the cab and as you can see by the reflection in the tailgate the paint is like glass. Painted running boards are protected by rubber step strips laid along the length of the board.

Planning your street rod carefully should mean you have developed an overall concept for your car. The previous chapter on Front End Treatment warned of the danger of going with a particular style 'just because it's the trend of the moment'. That same advice also applies to the rear end. Decide what style you want your car to be, and stick with it right through. Having settled on a style, don't pick up your tools yet, because there are still a few things to take into consideration.

For instance, you may have decided to go with a bumperless style front and rear. This makes for a clean appearance but also exposes your precious sheetmetal to greater risk of damage in parking lot 'skirmishes'. An alternative might be to keep the bumper but remake the irons to pull it closer to the body. Another popular trick, particulary with mid-'30s Fords, is to substitute a straight commercial bumper for the 'dipped' original. Other easily accomplished changes might include removing the spare wheel and its bracket and/or changing the

tail lights. But remember whatever you do, keep the style consistent over the whole car.

Let's take the rear lights option a couple of steps further. It may be that you have elected to go with the easy option and retain the original tail lights. However they are often not very effective due to small size, poor placement, low bulb brightness or poor reflectors. Aftermarket brighter bulbs are already available but you can also make quite a difference by using silver foil to line the inside of the tail light housing for greatly improved reflecting ability.

Next option is to change the lights altogether but if you go this way take care that your replacements aren't too small to be easily seen by following traffic and/or fit a third eye brake light for good measure. Should you decide to change the lights but don't want to mess up your precious bodywork try fitting them into an old bumper that you can paint to match the body or even incorporate them into the bumper brackets. This makes it easy to change to a different style again or maybe go back to the originals.

Third eye brake lights on sedans and coupes are usually easiest to fit in the lower part of the rear window. Sometimes though they can be very effective if incorporated into the body mould line. In similar fashion you could use the body roll around the back of the cabin section on roadsters and coupes or even incorporate it into the rear window surround on a roadster. Pickup trucks lend themselves to third eye brake lights mounted in the top rail of the tailgate or in the end of a 'solid' tonneau cover.

Next we'll turn our attention to fuel fillers. Again the solution to making yours look 'right' may be just as simple as tidying up the original pieces. Even just adding a milled aluminum cap will give an original filler a whole new appearance. Go one step further by using a hide-away fuel filler door from a late model car with a curved panel that matches your early fender or even move it into the rear quarter panel. Don't forget to retain the vent tube as well though, for easy filling.

Another option for the fender mounted filler, or one that is incorporated into the tail light stand like '35-'36 Fords, is to redesign a swing-away mechanism for the tail light so that the filler is completely hidden from view. This will take a little more work but the clean result will be worthwhile. Yet another alternative is to hide the fuel filler behind the license plate. Recessing the plate into the back panel of a large flat sedan helps to break up the expanse of panel and you can hide the fuel filler behind the recessed plate.

Some states require fenders on all street rods so you might as well make them look as good as you can. Phillip Pieper achieved a great result on his T bucket by using aluminum sheet for the cycle fenders, but he went one step further by milling highlight grooves into them. Even the mounting bracket has been given the milled highlight treatment for added detail. More milled mastery appears in the exhaust hanging bracket that also does duty as a tie bar for the Jaguar rear end.

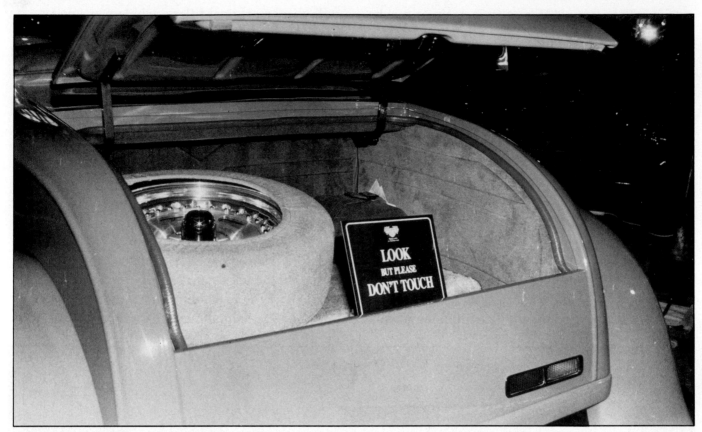

One disadvantage to using fiberglass bodies is finding a way to finish off the raw edges of panels where they join. Glen McGinnis overcame this problem on his Model A roadster by using the simple edging trim from around door openings to clean up the inside edge of the drip rail in the trunk. It looks so neat you hardly even notice what has been done.

The final thing we will deal with in our Rear End Treatment is the exhausts. This is another area where simplicity is often the best approach. Just getting them even, the same height and length, etc., makes a big difference to the balance of a car. Try experimenting with placement and remember there do not have to be two evenly spaced outlets at the rear. Try two pipes together on one side, one large diameter pipe, with or without megaphones, etc.. To test different styles and placements just hang lengths of exhaust tubing under the rear end and change them around. Then go with the style you like best and that suits the overall style of your car when you make the finished product.

Now it's time to go rear end style reviewing in pictorial form.

In the Front End Treatment chapter we showed you the front of Ian Hickey's '35 Ford coupe, now here's the rear. Tail light stems have been shortened and the bumper irons reshaped to pull the bumper in closer to the body. The result is a more compact, solid looking car.

This Australian '34 Chevy ute owned by Ron McDonald has some tidy detail work around the rear end. These utes generally have a very square, blunt finish at the lower end of the bed but Ron has really tidied his up by making up a cover panel that provides a mounting place for the tail lights and recessed license plate and also blends nicely through to the bottom of the rear fender. Rubber chain covers on the tailgate will prevent paint scratches, too.

There doesn't appear to be anything too special about the rear of John Katsanis' '32 Ford hiboy roadster until you focus on the license plate light. It has been made from a length of stainless steel tube capped at both ends and with a section milled out in the middle to house the light. Mounted like this it echos the shape and style of the tie bar between the frame horns to give the rear of the roadster an integrated but simple appearance. These license plate lights are available commercially.

The rear end of Tony Kuchel's '37 Ford club coupe displays a very clean, uncluttered appearance thanks to the removal of the original bumper and the tidy way the beavertail panel has been smoothed and blended to the rear fenders. The centrally mounted exhaust tips balance nicely with the license plate opening that accepts the plate from behind. Teardrop tail lights can be difficult to see in bad weather so Tony has mounted a pair of accessory brake lights in the lower sections of the rear windows where they aren't noticed thanks to a tinted strip in the glass — until you step on the brake and suddenly they're there!

This rear three-quarter view of Tony Kuchel's '37 Ford club coupe shows how important it is to stay with the one style from front to rear. See how the smooth all-paint look has been used to great effect on the hood sides, running boards, doors and trunk lid. Even a late model painted type mirror is used on the door to fit in with the overall concept.

Even resto-rods have clever ideas that you can learn from for your own project. Ian Aplin's '28 Dodge tourer is a show winner thanks to details like the Model A Ford rear bumpers that finish off the rear and combine well with the centrally mounted spare wheel. The bumper bracket also provides a convenient location to mount the radio antenna. Directional indicators are from a motorcycle.

The rear end of Aussie utes can be susceptible to damage because of the extra overhang and lack of bumper in stock form. Colin Bates provided his '36 Ford ute with some extra protection by making a robust chromed steel bumper that also provides a mounting place for the license plate and rear turn signals which echo the design of the '36 headlights. The rodders favorite, '39 Ford teardrop tail lights keep the rest of the rear end clean and tidy looking.

If your Model A street rod has a smooth, high tech style the original tail lights will only interrupt that smooth styling. The owner of this tourer kept his rear end styling really smooth by adding a clean extra lower panel under the rear of the body and mounted the tail lights there. Mounting the license plate under the rear also allows it to perform its function without being too prominent.

Another smooth tail light idea on a Model A tourer is shown here. Brad Lower used parts of a late model Falcon tail light lens and fitted them into the fender from the inside through slots that leave the surface of the lens flush with the surface of the fender. The upper two are for the tail light and brake light while the lower two are turn signals.

Ken Baker's '28 Model A Ford closed cab pickup retains all of its original factory style at the rear but there are a couple of simple updates that add a finishing touch. Neat milled aluminum covers have been used to fill the ends of the pickup bed mounting frame and mounted directly underneath them is a pair of accessory turn signal lights that are clearly visible when in operation yet don't look out of place in this position. Other things to note are the sturdy but removable tow hitch and nicely detailed Jag rear end. Mid mounted exhaust outlets are also square finished in keeping with the rest of the rear end styling.

You have to look really hard to pick some of the details of Frank Arone's '33 Ford Vicky convertible. While it appears to have no tail lights there is actually a single full width lens moulded into the very lower edge of the smooth rear apron. Eliminating the fender welting is another trick that makes an early Ford look much cleaner and Frank has further refined his street rod by flush mounting the license plate into the apron and adding a flip out fuel door high in the middle of the rear panel.

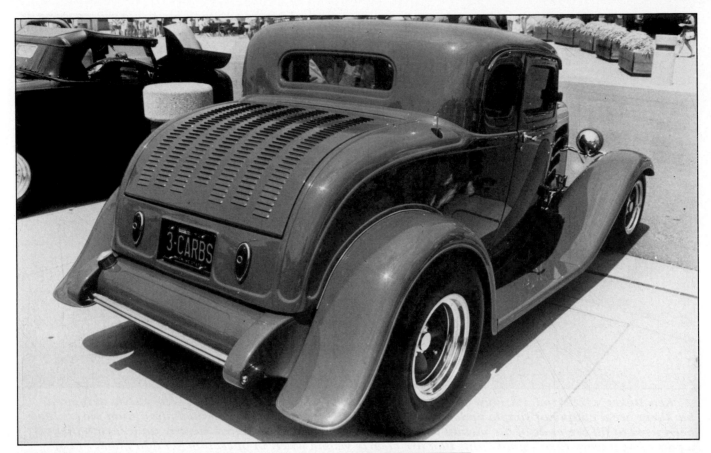

Above: Take a while to soak up the many styling touches incorporated into this '32 Ford five window coupe owned by Dave Summers of Kansas City. Dave has achieved the classic "hot rod" look by filling the rear deck with louvres, tunnelling the radio antenna, recessing the license plate into the lower panel complete with moulded bead around the opening and fitting traditional '39 Ford teardrop tail lights with blue dot lenses. You probably also noticed that Dave left the bumpers off and chopped the top. Overall stance of the vehicle and the wheel/tire combination and fit is perfect for this style of car. Think I'll just gaze a little longer!

If there is one thing about current street rod styling that always looks good it is the trend toward cleaning up the overall early styling lines of early bodies. Here is a good example where the rear bumper has been pulled in closer to the body, the stock tail lights and trunk handle removed and a new fuel filler door blended into the rear fender. No fender welting is used and the three rear lights are flush mounted with the panel surface.

Ford never made a roadster pickup in '39 but that hasn't stopped Wayne and Diane Young making their own. The bed essentially retains the original styling elements but it has been substantially updated through the use of a ribbed tonneau cover that matches the tailgate. Slotted openings reveal the matching tail lights and third eye brake light and the original type bed reinforcing rails have been given a fully moulded finish. A flush mounted fuel filler door is blended into the rear fender.

Everything is made to look like it belongs on the rear of this '34 Chevy roadster owned by Jody Guirino of Dayton, Ohio. Note how the tail lights match the body reveal line across the lower edge of the rear panel which in turn has been blended into the quarter panels. No fender welting is used to keep everything looking nice and clean, there's no external handle on the rumble seat and the third eye brake light has been cleverly incorporated into the milled aluminum rear window surround.

The large flat expanse of a '35 Ford flatback sedan can appear too blank if completely cleaned of all original fittings. Here's a good example of how to overcome that problem in style. Jerry Horsely has fitted slotted tail lights in the lower edge of the rear panel along with a nicely flush mounted license plate. Higher up the panel the third eye brake light echos the shape of the rear window. A neat double pinstripe just below the beltline also helps to break up the expanse of red paint.

Not many '37 Chrysler Imperial coupes make it to street rod status but that doesn't mean they can't be just as exciting as any other bodystyle. John R. Holland eliminated the bumpers from the rear end of his example, added slotted tail lights, flush mounted fuel filler door and a recessed license plate for a nice clean overall appearance.

Refining the styling of the rear of a '33 Willys coupe can be quite a challenge as there are so many different shapes to contend with. Bob Ida has done well here by incorporating a third eye brake light and rear license light into what appears to be a stock original tail light in the centre of the spare wheel recess. New larger tail lights have been custom made and shaped to create a continuation of the lower edge of the rear panel while underneath a large milled bracket acts as a carrier for the four exhaust pipes.

Le Roy Welch owns this '35 Chevy roadster that also displays a very simple but clean approach to rear end styling. Milled aluminum tail light housings have been incorporated into the lower edge of the rear panel but they have been painted to match the body, as has the recessed milled aluminum license plate bracket. Perfectly fitting rear fenders need no fender welting and the exterior rumble seat handle has been eliminated.

If a modern custom rod style is what you seek you will stop here for a while to check all the detail changes on Paul Maurer's really low Model A Ford coupe from Toronto, Canada. The wheel wells have been eliminated by making the entire quarter panel one smooth panel from front to rear and top to bottom. Elaborate grille style tail light openings and recessed plate look modern and the large single oval exhaust outlet is a truly individual touch. Adding to the smooth integrated look is the chopped and filled roof and the rounded corners on the deck lid.

The rear end of this '33 Plymouth coupe has responded well to a clean up of the original styling elements and the addition of some late model style tail lights flush mounted in the lower panel. The recessed license plate adds a little relief to the smoothed off styling and the custom made rear apron replaces the stock rear bumper and its associated mounting brackets.

Hiboy style '34 Ford tudor has some interesting styling elements including a high mounted third eye brake light that actually sits between two ribs that extend along the length of the roof. The tunnelled radio antenna is a nostalgic touch while the slotted tail lights are more modern. They are mounted in an add-on panel that echos the lower body reveal. The recessed license plate is accentuated by nostalgic pinstriping. Notice the bolt-in towing hitch that can obviously be easily replaced with a standard tie bar when the trailer isn't required.

Neat details around the exhaust outlets of this '33 Ford roadster. The lower section of the rear apron has been relieved to clear the twin exhaust outlets but the standard mould line continued around the cut outs so they look "factory". The fuel filler has been eliminated and tiny turn signals mounted to the lower outer edges of the apron.

Australian coupe utes make great street rods but their rear end styling treatment from the factory was basic at best. Here's a nice example of how well they can respond to some extra work and this '38 Chevy version now resides in Utah. The rear of the pickup bed area has been filled and moulded so that it flows back to the fenders with a smooth roll pan incorporated. The space between the fenders under the bed has also been filled with a matching panel that really finishes off the styling. Neat rectangular tail lights and a license plate recessed into the tailgate complete the picture.

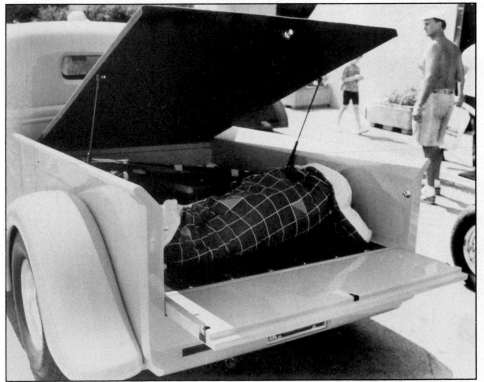

There's a lot to see in this '35 Ford pickup but for now we'll concentrate on the tailgate and tonneau cover. Three bearsclaw type latches have been incorporated into the tailgate. The outer two secure the gate itself while the middle one secures the hard tonneau cover which is made from aluminum, covered in material and supported by late model gas rams.

Buick owners rejoice! It's hard to imagine how the rear of a '39 Buick Special convertible could be refined any better than this example owned by Jim and Jodi Flett of Vancouver B.C., Canada. The rear bumper has been pulled right in close to the body, recessed flush mounted tail lights fitted and the trunk lid completely smoothed.

The all-paint theme has been well executed on this '39 Chev sedan owned by Jim Kalkes of West St Paul, Minnesota. Note how the rear bumper has been mounted closer to the body on custom made brackets that dip under the smoothed and rounded rear pan. The milled aluminum license plate bracket has been painted to match the body, as has the rear bumper. Recessed tail lights echo the shape of the dual exhaust outlets, a flush mounted fuel filler door has been fitted into the rear fender and a retractable radio antenna disappears into the body beltline.

"Duwop '39" is owned by George Nan of Madera, California and he has added several personal touches to his street rod. Of particular note is the side exiting dual megaphone exhaust, all-paint finish including the bumper, recessed license plate and flush mount fuel filler. Even the teardrop tail light surrounds have been painted and they are fitted with smooth look lenses.

Shortened bumper irons are a feature of the rear end of Gary and Sandy Woody's '37 Ford convertible sedan from Porterville, California. Mounting the tail lights to the bumper allows for future updating without involving bodywork. A recessed plate breaks up the expanse of the trunk lid and the twin centrally mounted megaphone exhausts leave no doubt that this is a hot rod.

Lots of subtle changes are evident on this '32 Ford hiboy roadster but you might have to look carefully to pick them all. This is obviously a fiberglass repro body as the side body reveals have been completely removed rearward of the cab section. The lower beaver panel is fully moulded in and the corners of the deck lid have been rounded. Look even closer and you will see the neat third eye brake light blended into the body reveal at the back of the cabin and the bolt-on lower finishing panel that carries the tail lights.

Here's some slick and individual styling changes made to the rear of a '40 Ford coupe. A large single oval exhaust oulet is used and highlighted by the simple nerf bar that also picks out the recessed license plate. Lenses for the tail lights have been custom made to follow the contour of the fender. Bold paint graphics add another dimension to this modern street rod.

Something to be careful of when opting for a modern rod style is that you don't lock yourself into a dating appearance as time goes by. Wayne Medlin of Boulder, Colorado shows us how you can overcome the situation. His '30 Model A coupe utilises a custom made pan that incorporates tail lights, a recessed license plate and quad exhaust outlets that all could be easily changed if required. Fenders have also been bobbed in hot rod style and a third eye brake light added to the rear of the cabin.

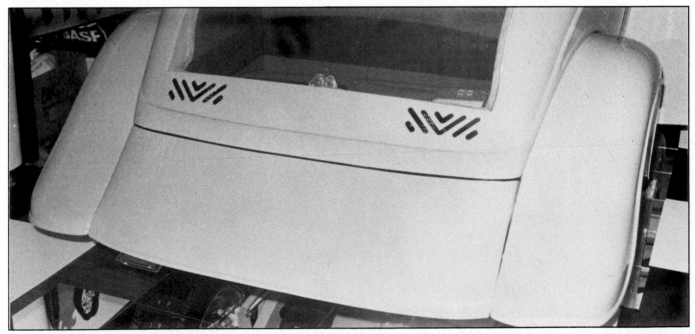

Glen McGinnis' '34 Ford coupe uses common accessory tail lights but you would never know because they are mounted behind elaborate looking cut outs in the rear body panel. The rest of the rear end styling is very clean and simple with just a single chromed oval exhaust tip on one side.

Dale Geary's '34 Ford coupe has thin Briz bumpers tucked in close to the body with smart bumper iron covers made to match the contour lines of the rear and painted body colour. Teardrop tail lights are recessed into the fenders and the license plate is recessed into the rear apron above a single centrally mounted exhaust outlet.

Smart two tone paint lends itself well to George Poteet's '34 Ford delivery which also features a smooth apron less fuel filler cap, no exterior door handle and a third eye brake light. Note also how the tail light bodies have been moulded directly to the fender.

Another '37 Ford with bumper mounted tail lights, this time on a tudor sedan owned by Dane Christensen. The third eye brake light mounted just below the rear window matches the styling of the other two and everything is painted to match the body. Relief from all the paint is given by bold graphic striping along the beltline. Note that in this case the stock bumper cutouts with rubber seals have been retained allowing for an easy return to standard but the irons have been shortened to bring the bumper closer to the body.

Third eye brake light on this chopped coupe has been mounted from inside the body so that its lens sits flush with the body surface. No frame is used and no means of retaining the light is visible from outside. The result is a nice tidy installation that looks good, yet remains simple.

A different approach to making a tonneau cover for a Model A roadster pickup is shown here. Made entirely from aluminum and form fitted to the bed it would be weathertight and it looks smart. It could be left as is in brushed finish or could be covered with material for a moulded fabric appearance.

Tony Correa's Australian '37 Chevy sedan has several custom touches that really liven up its appearance. The full width tail light is from an Australian produced Fairlane and has been neatly fitted into its own formed recess. Gas rams have been added to the trunk lid to hold it in the open position.

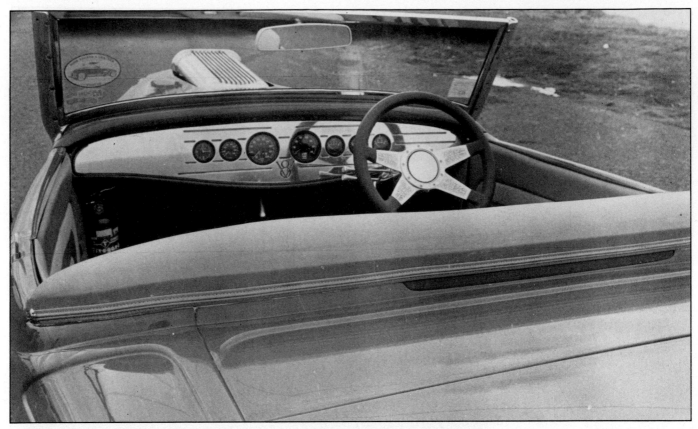

This close up photo shows how neatly the third eye brake light has been incorporatd into the upper body reveal on John Dyer's '32 Ford hiboy roadster. Making modern conveniences fit into the style of an early body is an art form in itself and this is an excellent example of how well it can be achieved.

Hot rodders can always come up with another clever idea. Here it's a nifty lift up license plate that reveals a mounting tube for a trailer hitch. In similar fashion the fuel filler door flips outward and at the lower edge of the rear end the rectangular tail lights match well with rectangular exhaust outlets. Owners are Patrick and Kathy Knight of Louisville, Kentucky.

Terry Tomasek put his '33 Ford cabriolet together in Omaha, Nebraska and incorporated this individual full width tail light across the top of the rear apron. It follows the shape of the apron completely to give a totally integrated appearance. Tunnelled into the centre is a deep recessed license plate with illuminating lights hidden behind holes down the sides of the recess. Close fitting panels mean fender welting is unnecessary, adding to the clean functional look.

Peter Quaife's '32 Ford hiboy coupe is very traditional in style but there are a couple of interesting features at the rear. Notice how the polished stainless steel exhaust follows the chassis rail very neatly and then gently drops away at the end. Clean and functional. No frame horn covers are used on this hiboy so the exposed ends of the body scallop where it clears the fuel tank make an ideal location for the neat aftermarket turn signals.

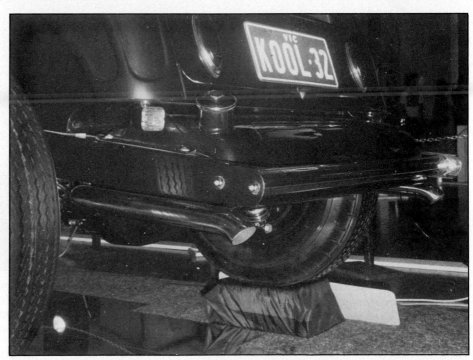

Rear view of this pickup truck reveals suicide doors, smooth all-paint appearance and solid tonneau cover. Tail lights have been incorporated onto the ends of the bed rails in stylish fashion while the third eye brake light is mounted in the top of the tailgate just above a nicely recessed license plate. Extra wide fenders indicate the rear end has been heavily tubbed to clear some serious rubber and the space between the fenders has been filled in with a cover panel. It's "FATNBAD".

Take away the stock bumper and its mounting slots, clean up the lower edge of the body and you have a whole new appearance for a '35 Ford coupe as evidenced by this photo of Robert Wilson's example. The license plate is tucked underneath out of the way and a pair of accessory turn signals are mounted to the underside as well. The finishing touch is a pair of round exhaust outlets centrally mounted under the bustle.

Hard to beat the styling elements incorporated into Barry Cook's '35 Ford coupe. Late model lenses have been flush fitted into the rear fenders on either side of the fender "peak" and the ribbed bumper has been mounted on shorty bumper irons to draw it closer to the body. Note how the illuminating lights for the recessed license plate have been hidden behind slots in the top of the recess. The fluted exhaust covers are decorative only and won't be blackened by the exhaust.

Look in the reflected images in the photo (right) and you can see where the real outlets are actually in the bottom of the tailpipe extensions. This car is loaded with similar features throughout.

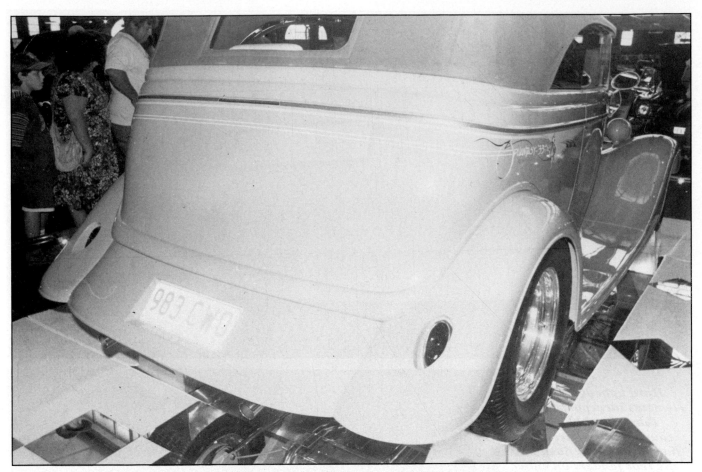

Look closely at the paint graphics and you will see how the third eye brake light has been incorporated into the rear of this '34 Ford phantom Victoria phaeton so well that it is barely noticed. Tear drop tail lights have been tunnelled into the fiberglass fenders and a recessed license plate added to the center of the rear apron. Everything else is very smooth and the rear bumper has been eliminated. Owner is Russell Wright from Brisbane, Australia.

Keep it plain, keep it simple and it will look good. "IB KOOL 1" because there is no rear bumper or cutouts in the body to distract your attention from the clean body lines. Likewise the fender welting has been removed and the license plate is self contained in its own bracket with illuminating light and third eye brake light.

This '36 Plymouth has been treated to some custom work at the rear to clean up the stock lines. The bumper has been discarded and tail lights mounted behind cut outs in the lower body panel for an updated appearance. Note the lockable flush mounted fuel filler door and color coded fender welting. Low mounted license plate is possibly retractable for cleaner appearance when parked at a show.

James and Michelle Wolk show us how tidy the rear end of a '37 Ford can look. Their convertible tudor version has tail lights and license plate all cleverly mounted on the bumper and its mounting irons which will allow them to update to another style in the future with minimum fuss. A really nicely fitted top of the right proportions is a make or break item on a car like this.

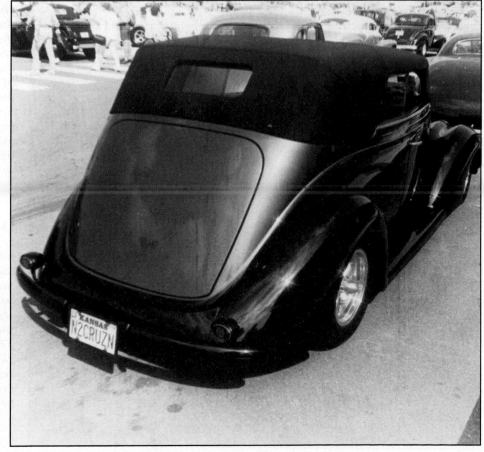

Here's another car that featured in the front end styling chapter and this photo shows that the rear end has been given the same treatment. A heavy chromed bumper has been custom made to protect the rear of the pickup bed and it dips down in the center to clear the license plate. Neat stainless steel brackets mount the stock type tail lights and the electrical wiring for these lights is hidden inside polished flexible covers.

The rear of John Portelli's '32 Ford tudor shows a distinct pro-street flavor with tubbed wheel wells and no rear bumper. Tail lights are flush mounted in billet aluminum housings and a competition style fuel filler is centrally mounted high in the rear panel. The stock '32 chassis rail extensions and fuel tank have been replaced with a '33/'34 style rear apron for a more integrated appearance.

Graeme Bevis opted for an ultra modern style with his '33 Ford coupe incorporating as much as possible from a late model donor vehicle. In keeping with the theme the body and fittings have been given an updated appearance too. Tail lights have been neatly flush mounted into the fenders without surrounds. The fender reveals around the wheel openings have been removed and a new style bumper made to follow the curvature of the body.

Side view of Graeme Bevis's '33 Ford shows how closely the bumper follows the body lines and shows more clearly how the reveals have been removed from the fiberglass fender openings. Fuel filler has been moved to the top of the rear deck and gas rams operate the trunk lid. There's also a late model latch used to keep the trunk closed.

Overall rear view of Don Langdon's '33 Ford hiboy coupe shows how well he has captured the early hot rod styling. Of particular note is the neat but very simple rear nerf bar which is made from a length of tube that has been curved to follow the shape of the rear of the body. Tail lights are '48 Ford with blue dots added.

In the front end styling chapter we showed you a photo of Graham Cowan's '34 Chevy roadster that uses a '35 Ford front bumper. Here's the same treatment given to the rear end and it suits the car perfectly. Recessed license plate and louvred apron let you know that this isn't a stock Chevy.

There are a couple of neat tricks incorporated into the styling of this '35 Ford coupe that really help reflect the clean custom look. The tail light staunchions have been shortened to pull the tail lights themselves closer to the body. Note how their final position aligns perfectly with the trailing edge of the fender. The bumper is an aftermarket Briz Bumpers ribbed item that is more slender than the original style and helps to give the car a lighter appearance. Stubby custom made mounting irons bring the bumper closer to the body for a more integrated appearance, a trick that works well on these models.

Finding a third eye brake light that suits the styling of your street rod can be tricky. You don't want it to look too much like an afterthought but you still want it to be effective. It would be hard to find one much more suitable than this example from a late model convertible that looks right at home mounted into the deck lid of a '40 Ford convertible.

A fully loaded small block Chevy engine dominates the engine bay of this Model A Ford roadster. Normally an engine so equipped would cause firewall interference problems but the problem has been overcome in this instance by reversing the stock Model A firewall and welding it back in place. The firewall still looks stock because it retains the original pressings but space in the engine bay is increased dramatically.

Personal taste will play a large part in the planning of your engine bay, particularly when it comes to choice of powerplant. Add together the choice of car you are building with the choice of engine to power the thing and you have a combination of factors that will have an almost infinite amount of influence on the way you design your engine bay and firewall.

Despite the foregoing factors there are still some basic measures that must be taken into consideration. Probably the most important of these is cooling. Nothing will cause you more frustration than to build a dynamite looking or sounding street rod if you can't fully enjoy it because of constant overheating problems. Hot rodders are ingenious when it comes to fitting something (particularly an engine) in a space where it wasn't designed to go. But in the case of a cramped engine bay all that ingenuity will be of little use if you can't also find a way to fit a radiator of suffi-

cient capacity to keep the engine cool.

First among your priorities in this area then should be careful selection of your running gear to suit the car of your choice, or to be more particular, the engine bay of that car.

Fortunately most early cars from the era that hot rodders select as their base car had engine bays that were of considerable size, so for the most part, getting the engine into the space isn't a major drama. Of course there are always exceptions to the rule but for the purposes of this book we'll assume that if you're building such a car you have the mechanical ability and experience to overcome such limitations. If not perhaps you should re-appraise your project before you get in too deep and give up on the project through frustration.

Now back to the subject at hand. While many late model engines will fairly readily fit into early engine bays there are often minor complications

This engine bay shot illustrates some neat but standard features like the way the indentation in the firewall of a '34 Chevy originally intended to accomodate the length of a six cylinder engine now provides clearance for the small block V8 distributor. It also has a neat three piece hood with internal latch release mechanism but the really interesting trick that doesn't immediatley catch your eye is the use of Velcro material as hood lacing. This looks right at home when being used for this purpose and doesn't leave untidy rub marks on the underside of the hood. Owners of the Chevy are Tom and Barb Hinderleider of Grayling, Michigan.

that call for hot rodding adaptability. Let me give you a couple of common examples. The most popular engine for use in street rods is undoubtedly the small block Chev. There are a few reasons for this. It is compact in design, readily available and inexpensive to rebuild. While its compact design makes this engine relatively easy to fit in most early engine bays it does have one fairly major shortcoming, that is the placement of its rear mounted distributor. More often than not this one factor will mean that modifications to the firewall are required for clearance. How effectively you make such modifications will have quite a bearing on the finished appearance of your engine bay so make sure you think them through thoroughly. Don't forget that whatever changes you make on this side of the firewall will also have

consequences on the other side, so think carefully. It may be that as a result you will opt to set back the whole firewall or a large part of it for clearance rather than just the small area around the distributor.

If you aren't using a small block Chev engine the next most obvious choice is the small block Ford. Again it is compact in design making it a good choice for early engine bays but it also has one fairly major shortcoming. While it does have a front mounted distributor, overcoming the firewall interference problem peculiar to Chevs in this area, the engine itself is longer resulting in firewall interference problems again, in this case from the heads. Once again the solution is to recess the firewall to suit and again the same criteria as applies to the Chev example now applies to the Ford.

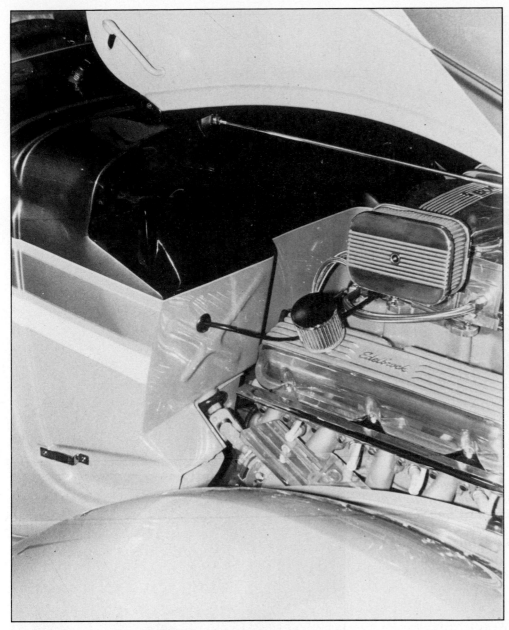

Barry Cook's '35 Ford coupe has a very tidy engine bay that is enhanced by the two tone paint scheme being carried through to the fire-wall. Although the firewall appears basically stock the second step forward at the bottom indicates it has actually been moved back several inches. It main-tains the stock appearance by retaining the standard pressings in the vertical face. Another detail item worthy of note in this right hand drive car is the milled alloy steering box cover complete with V8 logo.

There is another way of overcoming or min-imising this firewall interference problem when using a small block Ford engine but it does involve some mechanical changes. There are kits available that enable the use of a shorter water pump to gain a little space in front of the engine and so let you move it forward away from the firewall. You decide which is easier and less expensive for you, fit the shorty pump option or recess the firewall.

An additional consideration when using the Ford engine is the design of the oil pan. These engines have a front mounted oil pump and conse-quently the deep section of the oil pan is at the front. In some early cars this can cause interfer-ence between steering components and oil pan or when some independent front suspension systems are incorporated the oil pan will foul on the cross-member. Using a Bronco oil pan and pickup tube will help to overcome the situation but this is one area you should check thoroughly before you opt for the Ford engine.

Hot rodding has traditionally carried an aura of power with it so the V8 engine is bound to remain as the first choice of the majority of rodders, but if you would like some respite from the tight engine bay problems often associated with the use of V8 running gear take a look at the modern V6 engines. They're more compact in design, still have the attractive V configuration that dresses up well and best of all, they will usually fit an early

Robert Wilson's '35 Ford coupe features a mono-tone paint finish that is carried through to the engine bay. Anything that doesn't need to be exposed has been hidden including an LPG (propane) fuel system that hides under the large scoop. The firewall has been recessed deeply but smoothly to provide clearance for a big block Chevy engine.

All the original indentations and reinforcing ribs have been eliminated from the firewall on Dave Dorman's '34 Chevy roadster pickup by installing a completely new, flat firewall. This focuses all attention on the engine itself which in this case is detailed to compliment its surrounds. Look closely and you will see that the firewall has been painted with a random web effect over the body colour and the same unique detailing effect has been applied to the air cleaner! The body colour is turquoise and the webbing is light pink.

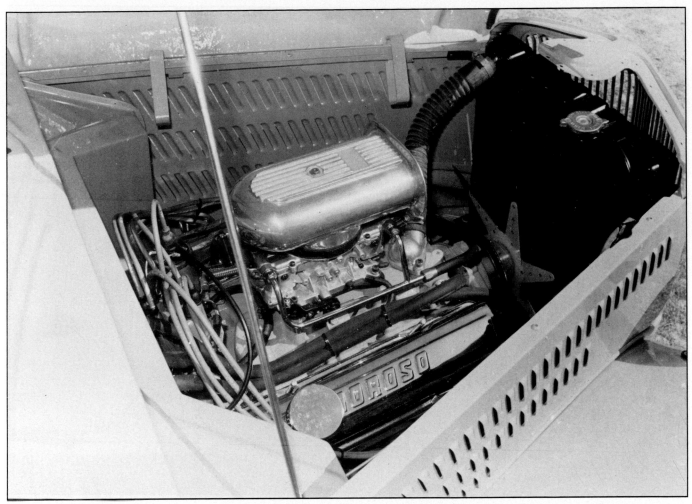

A stock bodied street rod doesn't have to be all original behind the sheetmetal to look and be a quality street rod. This '33 Ford uses a late model crossflow radiator mounted on end with a new filler neck mounted at the top. This requires custom bracketry to hold the radiator and grille in place but with careful planning it makes for a tidy engine bay. Take a look at the elaborate hinges on the three piece hood as well, done this way so that the top section of the hood can lift up and away as it is opened and thus prevent binding and paint scraping. A simple late model type latch is incorporated in the nearside panel to hold the hood closed in the down position.

engine bay with little, if any, modification to the surrounding sheetmetal.

Now let's go back to the other end of the engine bay for a closer look at ways to overcome potential overheating problems. Having found a way to stuff the engine of your choice into the available space you will now need to perform the same exercise with the radiator.

Often the very reason for massaging the firewall to fit your engine in place is so that you don't interfere with the original radiator. Good idea in most cases, especially if the original radiator is large enough to cool the engine of your choice and it is in good condition. Some early cars had quite efficient radiators but often they weren't pressurised, or if they were the pressures exerted on

them by the original engine weren't as great as your more recent running gear will produce. Therefore you will need to ensure that the core and soldered seams are in excellent condition and if necessary add a later model filler neck and pressure cap.

Sometimes there will be room to retain an engine driven fan but often it won't be positioned to best advantage. Fortunately in this day and age we have the availability of electrically operated thermostatically controlled fans that can be mounted directly to the face of the radiator for optimum airflow enhancement. In other words they work! Best of all they can be of 'pusher' or 'puller' design allowing them to be mounted either in front of or behind the radiator.

There are many custom made items on this phantom '34 Ford roadster pickup. Of particular note in this photo is the steel framework used to support the radiator and grille and to connect them to the firewall. The side rails also provide the mounting points for the three piece hood.

The lack of a good original radiator shouldn't be a deterrent to you completing your project. For the more popular makes reproduction radiators built to modern standards are readily available. They can be expensive, but in relation to the expense of the components they protect can be money wisely spent. Should your vehicle not fall into the 'popular make' category or if you feel the expense of a reproduction radiator isn't warranted, you will need to call on some ingenuity again.

Now it's time to arm yourself with a tape measure and go checking in a wrecking yard. As you go, keep in mind that the radiator you select won't only need to fit the space available, but it will also need the capacity to cool the engine you are using. Sometimes that will seem a daunting task as many of the modern cars use crossflow radiators that would seem to be impossible to fit in an early car. Not necessarily so! You see most

crossflow radiators will work just as well when tipped on their end. Sometimes you will need to alter the tanks and/or outlets but that isn't difficult and the only other requirement will be some form of mounting bracketry. If you have already progressed this far on your project the manufacture of a mounting system shouldn't be too much of a hurdle.

One advantage of using a non-standard radiator can be gained from the need to make some form of mounting system for such an installation. Often the mounting frame can be extended to incorporate the upper grille mount which sometimes is advantageous in that it overcomes the inherent weakness of an original factory grille installation. The grille is often the most valuable item on the car and anything you can do to enhance its ability to withstand the rigors of time and use is worth doing. Take this idea a step further and you could even

Street Rod engine bays don't come much cleaner than the one in this '32 Ford coupe owned by Bill Dixon. A smart cover has been custom made to hide the carburetor and its associated componentry and everything has been painted to match the body. Body reveals around the grille shell and firewall edges have been removed and a plain, flat firewall is only interrupted by the air conditioner drier. A smooth, three piece hood completes what is one very clean engine bay.

incorporate your radiator/grille mount into a complete frame for the engine bay that not only strengthens the whole structure but also gives you mounting points for a custom three piece engine hood. There are examples of just such a system in this chapter.

Using a radiator from a non-original donor car does require some careful assessing in one crtical area though. That is the placement of the outlets. The top and bottom outlets should always be opposite to each other so that the coolant has to traverse the whole radiator as it passes through. For similar reasons the pressure cap should always be mounted as high on the radiator as you can possibly manage. Sometimes this can be more difficult on an early car as the cap often interferes with the underside of the engine hood. The position of

that filler neck effectively determines the upper limit of the radiator's capacity so take the time to get it as high as you possibly can.

Every engine bay is different so there is little more that I can suggest here without getting down to specific cases. Better I think to take a look at how other rodders have gone about laying out the engine room of their projects. It's picture time again!

Fitting a small block Ford engine into a '27 Model T is quite an accomplishment! In Joylene and Wayne Eckert's coupe the whole firewall has been given a reverse dish to accomodate the length of the engine. Note the use of a remote mounted oil filter to overcome interference with the chassis rail.

Fitting a small block Ford engine in Ian and Jan Dawson's '34 Ford sedan was made easier by neatly recessing the firewall to clear the heads. This engine bay is made even tidier by the use of braided stainless steel fluid lines that are all routed and mounted in similar fashion. Study the way the radiator support rods have been custom made to provide clearance for the air cleaner.

At first glance you may not notice anything has been done to the firewall in this '35 Ford coupe but look again and you will see that the entire stock firewall has been moved back to provide more length in the engine bay. This provides plenty of clearance for the small block Ford engine and retains the original identity of the '35 Ford because the firewall still maintains its original pressings and shape.

John Portelli's '32 Ford tudor is powered by a big block Ford engine which would normally be a tight squeeze in this type of car. However John's tudor is a repro fibreglass body which makes it easy to incorporate a flat firewall, and consequently extra space, at the time of manufacture. Not only does the flat firewall afford more space for the engine but when painted body color it also makes the engine itself more prominent to the viewers eye. Detailing of cables, lines and leads helps to dress up the whole package. As a result John's '32 is a regular show winner and yet it is a driver too.

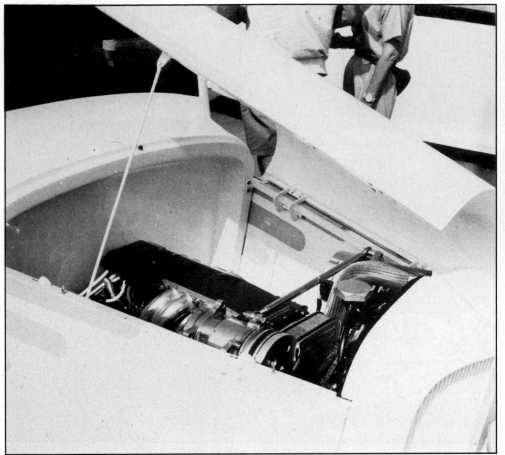

Even more space in the engine bay of a repro '32 Ford cabriolet can be gained by recessing the entire firewall area as Don McKinley has done here. The even contour of the opening makes the firewall appear stock. Note how the flat edge of the firewall has been retained and serves a purpose by providing an easy mounting spot for the hinge bar of the three piece hood. Also check out the scalloped paintwork both inside and outside the engine bay.

It's one thing to recess a firewall for engine clearance but it's another to make it look like it was meant to be that way. Alan Evans has done a great job on his '30 Model A Ford by recessing a large part of the firewall to clear a small block Ford engine. Take note of how Alan has rounded the edge of the opening to make it similar in style to the original outer edge of the stock firewall.

Access to the engine in an early street rod can be cramped in some instances but certainly not in this case. Hinge mechanism is fairly complex to allow the top section of the hood to tilt forward on this '34 Ford sedan but once in position it is held there by late model gas rams. Note the large but stock looking box added to the top section of the firewall. Such an addition could be used to house a number of items including air conditioning, wiring components, tools, etc. This area is otherwise just dead space and all these items take up valuable room inside the car so why not mount them here?

This Model A Ford has been fitted with a common readily available radiator and set behind a Deuce grille insert you wouldn't know the difference. A simple steel tube frame mounts both the radiator and the grille shell.

The stock battery location on top of the firewall in '37 Fords may have been handy for access but acid leakage would play havoc with the paint finish of the firewall. The space has been retained in this sedan but a tidy lid now covers the opening and instead of housing the battery it now acts as a hiding place for starter solenoid and fuse block.

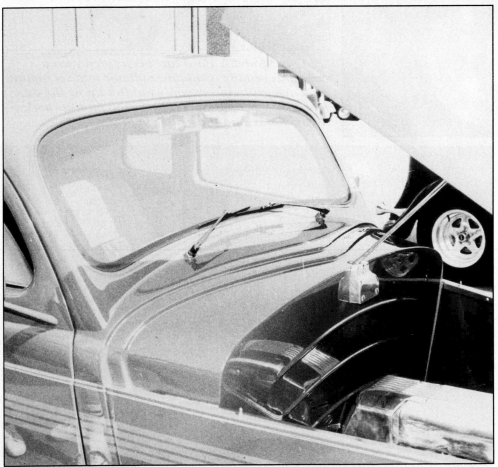

The hood on this '35 Dodge pickup didn't always open this way. Original four piece hood and grille have been welded together to make one unit that now tilts forward for access to the engine. The firewall area has been cleaned up extensively and small rubber buttons used in the cowl lacing holes for a tidier appearance.

Check out the firewall in this Dodge coupe. All the ugly original bumps have been replaced with a neat custom made firewall incorporating complimentary curved beads echoing the upper curve of the firewall. A centrally mounted latch also partly disguises the special indentation for the prop to sit in when the hood is open. Note the reflection of the engine in the highly polished but painted firewall.

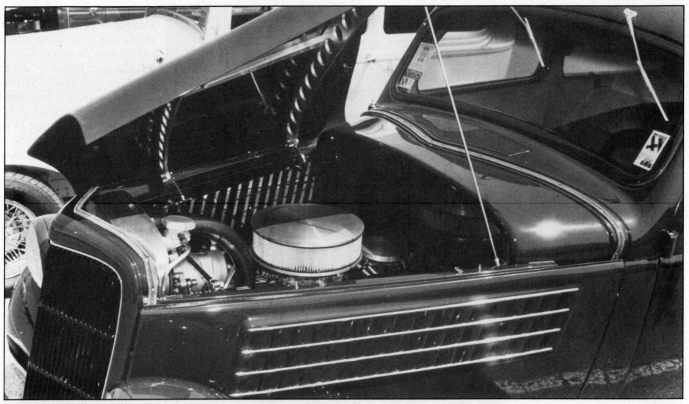

Tom and Jan Tollefson own this very tidy '35 Ford which has some clever additions under the hood. Of particular note is the milled aluminum upper hood support that connects to the side opening hinge. Another smart custom touch is the extension of the firewall all the way to the top of the engine bay. It has been all moulded in to look standard but the benefit is that it converts wasted space in the engine bay to valuable extra space under the dash for air conditioning, wiring, etc. inside the car.

Russell Wright's '34 Ford Victoria phaeton is packed full of custom features. Here we are concerned with the simple square tube frame to mount the radiator and grille but also note how the graphic paint detail extends under the hood to the top tank of the radiator which is smooth and painted body color.

Here's a really good example of how forward thinking can solve several problems at once. Glen McGinnis fitted a '32 grille shell to his Model A roadster and used a late model crossflow radiator mounted on its end to cool the blown small block Chevy engine. Glen has cleverly made the one bracket act as a fender tie bar, headlight mount and radiator support brace. Even mounts for the electric fan have been incorporated and it is all painted body color so that it blends in.

There's nothing too spectacular about the engine bay of this '34 Chevy sedan but notice where the radiator overflow tank has been mounted. Nothing dictates that it has to be alongside the radiator so why not mount it on the firewall?

If you have retained much of the original styling of your early Ford based street rod it often looks better if you can keep the firewall as original looking as possible. That has been done in this case but more clearance was required for the Chevy distributor. Rather than set back the entire lower half of the firewall this owner has neatly scallopped out a semi-circle immediately adjacent to the distributor. All of the original firewall pressings remain intact and the engine bay has a more factory original appearance than might otherwise be the case.

Another basically stock early firewall, this time in a right hand drive '46 Chevy coupe. The original six cylinder engine fitted to these cars required a depression in the centre of the firewall to accommodate their length and now it is perfectly suited to providing some additional clearance around the V8 distributor. Brake master cylinder and booster has been painted the same as the bodywork for a fully integrated appearance.

Study the front of Kevin Lewis' '34 Ford tudor very carefully and you will discover an amazing array of modern convenience items all nicely blended into the early bodystyle. Windshield glass has been fitted flush with the body and glued in modern car style, triple wipers are used for maximum wet weather vision and modern external rear view mirrors have been painted to match the body. Note the tiny washer jets mounted either side of the cowl vent and the demister outlets inside the windshield.

Getting in, getting out and seeing where you're going are all basic things we do when using a car of any type, but when it comes to street rods there's no reason to treat each of these aspects as mundane. With most early cars, as frequently used for rebuilding into street rods, the original means of access was never really given much thought. A door was a means of getting in and out and was usually designed to do that with a minimum of fuss. As long as it fitted into the general overall design of the car little thought was given to updating its efficiency of operation until relatively recent times.

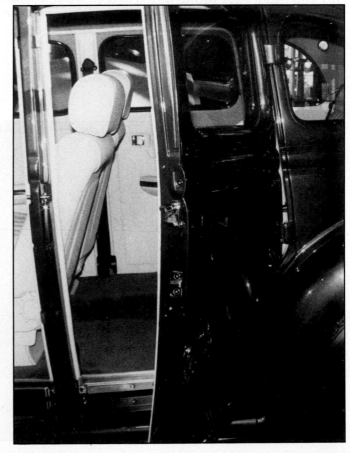

Fitting late model burst-proof door latches to early doors is a great benefit in two ways. It makes the car safer in the event of an accident as the door will be less prone to fly open and it also means the door is held in place firmly, eliminating rattles that can develop in conventional tongue style latches. Graeme Urquhart used small burst-proof latches in his '35 Ford sedan and also fitted recessed late model handles to the inside and outside of the doors. The exterior handles are painted body color so they blend in with their surrounds.

Here's an example of late model burst-proof door latches fitted to an early Model A roadster door. These doors aren't very wide so Phil Air provided more space in his by extending a box section to accommodate the latch. This box section extends all the way to the leading edge of the door and also incorporates the internal door release mechanism. The whole section has been made a highlight of the door panel and consequently no longer looks like an "add-on".

Hot rodders are always on the lookout for ways to improve their cars both for appearance and safety. Doors are an obvious area where just a little thought and mechanical ability can make quite a substantial difference to both those qualities with relatively little expense and inconvenience. The two main items on the list of improve-

ments that can be made to doors are the latches and the hinges.

Most early latches were of your basic tongue and wedge design which work okay when in good condition. However once they get a little worn the rattles set in with a vengeance and adjustment becomes almost a waste of time. Fortunately modern cars have what we know as the burst-proof or bears claw door latch mechanism which is relatively easy to adapt to early cars.

There are a couple of benefits to using burst-

Normally it is very difficult to fit burst-proof door latches to a Model A tudor door because the window glass would interfere with the location. Russell Arthur has overcome the problem on his delivery by moving the rear edge of the glass forward in a channel section that is painted to match the door and consequently is barely visible. Modern door handle has also been cleverly blended with early base so that the handle still looks authentic even though it is now push-button operated.

Another example of late model latches fitted to the door of a repro fiberglass '34 Ford coupe. Nothing special about that in these days but look closely for the external door release, it's located on the window rail alongside the glass where it could pass for an internal door lock release except that it is on the outside of the glass. This also satisfies the legal requirement for an external, mechanically operated door release that is required in some states and countries.

proof latches. Not only are they safer because they overcome the earlier design's tendencies to fly open in an accident, and sometimes while just driving down the road, they also tend to hold the door firmly in the one position. The old tongue and wedge design will allow the door to 'bounce' up and down in its opening, especially if the hinges are a bit worn, and the result is more annoying rattles.

Most late model door latch mechanisms also feature internal releases that are recessed into the door panel and these also lend themselves well to incorporation in an early street rod interior. Couple them with a neat arm rest and you have both comfort and style.

Nobody ever said the door latch mechanism must go into a car a certain way round. Andy Robinson fitted his '32 Ford five window coupe with late model burst-proof latches but he mounted the main latch in the body and the "posts" in the doors. You can see that in the far side of the car in this photo but look at the near side and you will also see how Andy has incorporated a small square release button just below the quarter window where it remains flush with the surrounding sheetmetal.

Ken Baker's Model A closed cab pickup retains original type door latches but look below the latch and you will see a tapered teflon block that guides the door into position in the opening via a similarly tapered steel locater. This device is from an International Truck and is ideally suited to the Model A.

Recent years have seen the advent of remote locking systems in late model cars and here's another convenience facility that rodders are increasingly adapting to their early cars. Not only are they fitting the remote locking facility though, often today's rodders are using the same technology to fit electronic door release mechanisms which mean the exterior door handle can be done away with altogether. Use caution if you contemplate fitting such a system to your own rod though as such electrically activated door latches are illegal in some states, where some mechanical form of opening device is required, supposedly in case of emergency access that might be required in an accident situation. Someone obviously forgot to tell the bureaucrats that in an accident serious enough to require emergency access there are usually no windows left in the car!

Hinges have formerly been given little attention in the rodding world apart from reconditioning the original system to work as efficiently as possible,

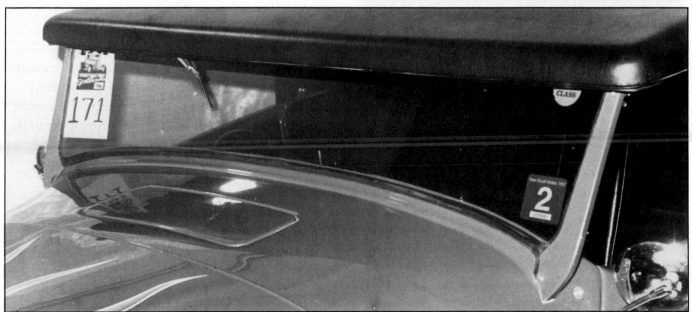

If you don't have an original set of windshield posts for your '32 Ford open car you can always custom make a pair like those used here. They have been shaped similarly to the originals but are much more simple in design. No windshield frame is used and the inside edge of the posts has a groove to hold the glass in place. At the lower edge a strip of rubber channel is used to support the glass across the top of the cowl.

Narrow ribs down the centre of the filled roof of this '32 Ford tudor owned by Phil Goller lead your eyes to the very neatly fitted windshield glass. The glass has been glued in place as is done on late model vehicles and a neat trim bead fitted around the edge gives it just enough definition. Phil's tudor is painted black all over including the windshield wiper which makes it less visible to the casual viwer. Note that the door handles have been given the same treatment.

which often isn't all that good at all. The advent of the hidden hinge has brought this aspect of rod building into the 21st century as well with after-market manufacturers offering a range of kits and hinges to suit almost any car. Be warned though that almost without exception fairly major body-work is required to fit hidden hinges. Of course you don't have to use the readily available after-market hinges to perform this change on your street rod either. Check out the small foreign made cars of today and you just might find a hinge system that can be adapted to your early car. Get them from a wrecking yard and the price will be right too.

Now let's turn our attention to the vision side of this section. Again it has been fairly usual up to this point in time to simply reproduce or replace the original windscreen and its associated fittings

with more of the same, albeit new or rebuilt. That can be a relatively expensive operation, especially if your car had a separate, chromed windscreen frame. Modern technology has come to the rescue again in this area with rodders benefitting from the trend to stick-in windscreens that eliminate the original frame altogether. It's a trend that we're bound to see more of in the future.

Associated with the vision aspect of street rodding is the accessory items that give you a clear view of the road. Here we're talking about windshield wipers and rearview mirrors in partic-ular. In too many cases the average home builder puts plenty of thought and work into his project only to let it down by not paying attention to the details in this area.

For instance, it is quite common to see a superbly finished street rod that just falls short of

Here's another '32 Ford that has been given slightly different treatment in the windshield area. In this case the windshield frame has been retained for a more original appearance but notice how you don't see any sealing rubber protruding from the edges. This makes for a much tidier installation and painting the frame in body color works really well.

Vision from inside this '32 Ford tudor is greatly enhanced by the elimination of the original windshield frame and gluing the glass directly into the stock height opening. The inner edges of the glass have been painted black to make it all look even and late model trimming bead fills the gap between the metal and glass. Removing the wiper blades while the car is on display is another trick that makes any rod appear much cleaner and tidier than would otherwise be the case.

When it comes to windshield wipers you won't find a much tidier or more efficient sytem than this triple version from a Nissan Patrol four wheel drive fitted to Kevin Kendall's Model A Ford tudor. The compact design of the pivots allows them to be easily mounted in the Model A header panel and when viewed from normal positions the whole wiper system is hidden by the sunshade. Look closely and you will see that Kevin has even included windshield washers in the header panel as well, one at each end.

'perfect' because the windshield wiper blades rest at awkward angles on the glass. Take a little more time to select parts that can be made to better fit your car and blend in more with the overall design. Again late model cars can often be the source of a neat wiper setup that could be easily adapted to your early car. They will work efficiently and usually come with inbuilt switch gear that automatically 'parks' the blades at the top or bottom of their throw. Play with combinations of blades until you find a pair that will 'park' parallel with the top or bottom of the windshield and they won't be anywhere near as noticeable as blades that must be left resting partly across the glass.

Often the particular design of an early car or

the placement of the wipers makes it hard to achieve a pleasing result. There's still another option left open to you, especially for when the car is on static display. Once you park the car in such a 'show' situation remove the blades before you leave to check out all the other rods and even fit little colour coded plastic covers over the drives. You just might find all the other rodders are checking out your car because it looks so clean and tidy, when all you did was remove the wipers!

In some states and countries it is now a legal requirement that your street rod be fitted with such modern conveniences as windshield washers and demisters. Don't shudder at the thought of trying to fit such items to your car. They can be fitted in

Fat fendered Ford fans will immediately pick this as a '35 Ford windshield but there are some important differences to an original '35. Robert Wilson has chopped his coupe and painted the frame to match the body. He has also moved the wipers from their standard position above the windshield and mounted them in the cowl. Note how the bend in the wiper drive arm also allows the blades to park level with the lower edge of the glass. It all adds up to a tidy but efficient installation.

such a way as to be unobtrusive if you just use a little intelligence.

Many early cars have original equipment that lends itself to conversion for hiding such things as the windshield washers. Let me give you a typical example. Frequently the original fuel tank on a Model A Ford is not used when the car is rebuilt as a street rod but often the original cap is retained. What better place to hide your washer outlets than in the cap with the finger grips drilled as outlets. You can even cut the bottom out of the tank and mount the washer bottle inside with filling access through the original fuel cap! In fact one of my own street rods features this very arrangement but with an accessory outlet mounted just to the rear of the hood hinge pivot where it is hardly noticed, especially since it is painted the same colour as the body.

The same theory applies to the fitting of a demisting system although this is sometimes a little more difficult to achieve in bodies that didn't

have a large dash. In cars built from the mid-thirties onwards though it shouldn't be a real problem. Study the way the factories fitted such demisting systems to late model cars and you will soon come up with a way to achieve the same result in your early rod.

When it comes to rear view mirrors individual choice must take a leading role. Still there are some basic rules to remember. It is surprising how many rodders just fit a mirror in the most convenient position with little thought to the possibility that it might be right in the driver's line of vision when negotiating heavy traffic. That could lead to a nasty accident which is the last thing you want in your street rod. Look for more options and you will find a better place to mount your mirrors where they won't intrude on the overall style of the car, but will still perform their important function of keeping you in touch with your surroundings.

The number one important thing to be aware of

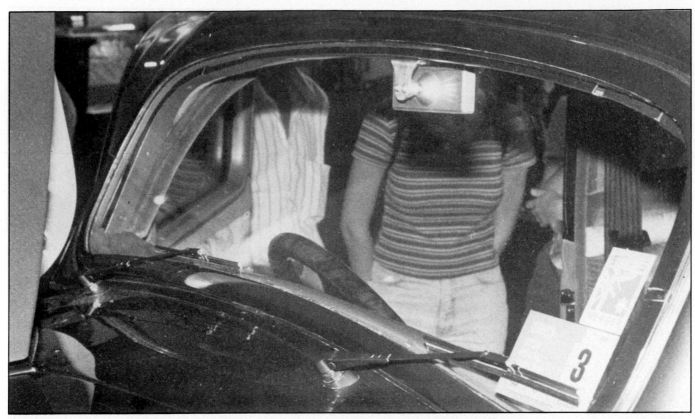

Barry Cook's '35 Ford coupe is another fat fendered street rod that makes use of a wiper system mounted below the windshield rather than the stock position above the glass. Both wipers and the windshield frame are painted body color and the wiper arms are shaped such that the blades park horizontally at the bottom of the glass.

Painting the windshield frame body color and mounting the wipers on the cowl also works on '34 Fords like Ian and Jan Dawson's sedan. Many small foreign cars have wiper systems that can be adapted in this way and their compact size usually means little modification is needed to fit them to an early body.

At first glance you might think this Model A Ford roadster doesn't have any windshield wipers at all! Look carefully though and you will see that there is a narrow gap left across the top of the cowl immediately in front of the windshield. Down in there are the wiper blades, completely hidden from view until you switch them on. The windshield is also rectangular in shape which should make it easier to replace. Notice how the custom made windshield posts have been moulded to the cowl and they are slotted to accept the glass without the need for any separate frame.

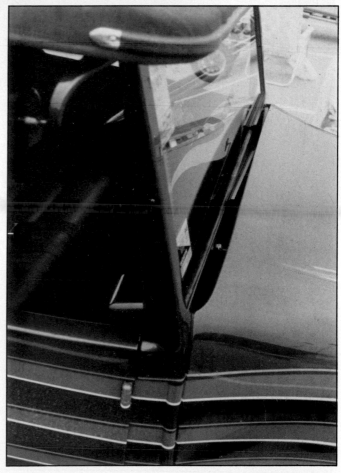

when it comes to mirrors is not to just hang them on the door because you have to have them. Try to select a style of mirror that will blend in with the style of your car and decide whether they would be better chromed, made from billet aluminium or maybe even painted to match the body. When it comes to access and vision it's the details that make the difference.

How many '40 Ford coupe owners would recognise this roofline? It looks vastly different to a standard '40 coupe because the top has been mildly chopped and the B pillar slanted forward at the top. A late model moulded style rear vision mirror and V-butted windshield glass are further refinements that make the "Bates 40" stand apart from the rest.

When your handiwork is this clever you might as well display it. One-piece lift off roadster roof has been designed to look like a folding top but it has been fully lined inside. Exterior mirrors and the complete wiper system has been mounted in the roof so that it comes off with it. Wiring for the wipers has a disconnection plug incorporated at the back of the roof.

Climbing into a T bucket that doesn't have opening doors can be quite a chore, especially if the car also has side pipes. Adding a chromed step plate to the exhaust hanger as shown here makes getting in and out much easier and the step looks right at home on this style of car.

George Poteet's '34 Ford "coupe/delivery" is a one-of-a-kind street rod that is further refined by eliminating the external door hinges and painting the running board to match the lower half of the body. Also note how the external rear view mirror has been moulded onto the leading edge of the door.

Many modern features have been used to update the trunk area of this Model A Ford coupe. Custom made hinges are much tidier than the original items and modern gas rams hold the lid in the open position. A stainless steel gas tank and battery box leave the inside clean and tidy. Neat little rubber bumpers at the bottom corners of the trunk will prevent squeaks and rattles when the trunk is closed. Note the tapered, flush fitting fuel filler door added to the quarter panel and the small modern latch mechanism that is triggered from the driver's seat.

Bill Robinson's Model A Ford tudor is full of clever ideas. Of note here is the flush fitting windshield glass that eliminates the original frame. The glass is glued in place as on modern cars. Note also that the lower corners of the windshield have been rounded so that they match the rounded corners of the side window glass. The roof has also been filled and the visor welded on instead of being held in place with screws.

It may not be readily apparent, but there have been numerous changes made to the door and windshield areas of Ron Smits' '39 Chevy sedan. The roof has been chopped and the windshield glass is now glued in place as on late model cars. The centre divider has been eliminated and the two pieces of glass butted together for a clean, uncluttered look. Turn your attention to the door and we can see more late model goodies blended into the styling in the form of recessed door handles and the rear view mirror. The leading corner of the window area has been filled in to provide a mounting point for the mirror and the original quarter vent window eliminated. It all adds up to one smooth package that all works together.

Think the trunk area of Jim Haworth's Model A coupe looks bigger than usual? You're right! Easy access to the trunk area has been afforded by incorporating the rear lower panel into the trunk lid. It's a whole new piece that extends from the floor all the way up to the rear of the cabin. Note the shorty gas rams used to hold the lid in the open position in conjunction with the custom made "overcentering" hinges. Even the heaviest loads could be placed in this trunk and there is almost no risk of damaging the body while doing so.

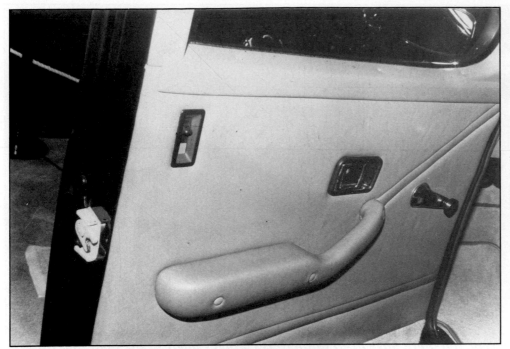

At a quick glance you might be forgiven for thinking you are looking at a late model car door. In fact this is a '34 Chevy sedan door that has been cleverly equipped with a combination of late model fittings by owner Geoff Hope. Burst-proof latches are from a VW as are the slide locks and the internal release mechanism. The window winder handle and the armrest are also donor items from late model vehicles. Careful planning makes it all appear standard.

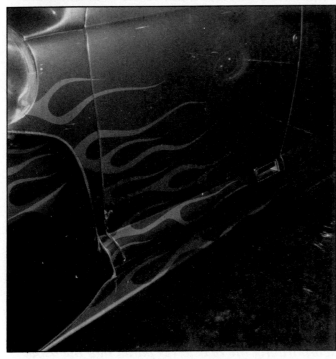

Above: Who says the door handles must be in the middle of the door. The side of this '48 Ford sedan is kept cleaner because the door release handles have been mounted in the return mould at the bottom of the door where they are hardly noticed.

Right: Same goes for the latch mechanism on this Model A door. Placing the latch low down on the door like this overcomes the problem of the door glass interfering with the latch location. The glass remains standard Model A but the late model burst-proof latch is still incorporated.

INTERIORS

How much you enjoy your street rod will largely depend on how comfortable it is to travel reasonable distances in the vehicle. Combine all the other factors that have a bearing on the finished product and it sometimes becomes very difficult, if not impossible, to build comfort into such a car. Let's face it the fact that you are using an early body style for a start restricts to what degree you can design an interior that provides function and comfort.

The next factor that will have a bearing on the interior of your street rod is the actual style of the car overall. This one keeps cropping up in every chapter of this book, doesn't it? It is the number one important factor though, in governing whether your car will be a balanced package that reflects the desires of its owner.

Take a typical example. You may have decided that pro-street is the style for you with killer engine and huge wheel tubs in the rear. Naturally such a car will also have a full rollcage and all the other competition appointments that go with the image. So be honest with yourself, it is very unlikely that such a car is going to be able to feature much in the way of comfort. Perhaps in this case that's not such a high priority as such a car will have limited practical touring ability. However if you are hopeful of combining a pro-street style rod with interior comfort built in you would be well advised to think again. It's highly unlikely to work out that way.

Okay, so now you have decided that yours will be a practical, down to earth street rod that could be driven every day of the week and on long jaunts to distant rod runs as well. It's not going to just happen. Planning is needed in this department just as much as it is in any other part of your project. I've already mentioned the restrictions that automatically apply just because you're using an early body. When it comes to fitting modern components such as seats, air conditioning/heaters entertainment systems and so on into that early body you are very quickly going to learn more about those restrictions. Being an ingenious rodder you will just as quickly find a way to overcome those same handicaps though, won't you?

If you need a little help, that's where this book comes into the picture. That's why you bought it in the first place, right? Featured on these pages are ideas galore from other rodders on how they

Study Gavin Poulish's Model A roadster pickup interior for a while and you will see several clever innovations. Late model burst proof door latches have been fitted in reverse fashion. The latch itself is mounted in the quarter panel with the release handle beside the passengers shoulder. The narrow Model A roadster door now only has to accommodate the stud part of the latch. The pocket sewn into the door trim is always a handy place to put maps and other travel requirements while on the way to a rod run. Note also how the roadster top is made to look like it folds but is in fact a one-piece lift-off arrangement that is completely lined on the inside. Snug fitting side curtains would make this roadster as weathertight as a coupe.

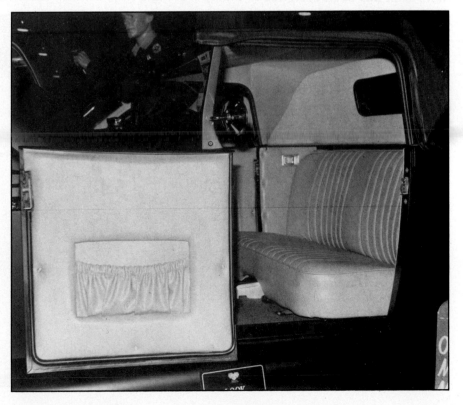

Who says interior trim has to be boring? This Model A roadster pickup uses contrasting black and red vinyl for a stylish interior design. The really fine cut pile carpet on the floor is also red and usually lines the floor of a Jaguar. Once again late model burst-proof door latches are fitted but this time in the conventional manner with the stud on the pillar and the latch meachanism in the door. Note how the door trim has been designed to incorporate and hide the latch mechanism when the door is closed.

Few street rods have an interior that is as luxurious as Graeme Urquhart's '35 Ford sedan. The seats are readily available mass market Ford items but they have been recontoured and trimmed in Rolls Royce fashion for a much more up-market end result. Armrests incorporate the electric window switches and inside door releases and they feature veneer inserts that match the steering wheel. Worth noting here too is the way the base of the seats have been completely covered in for a totally finished appearance.

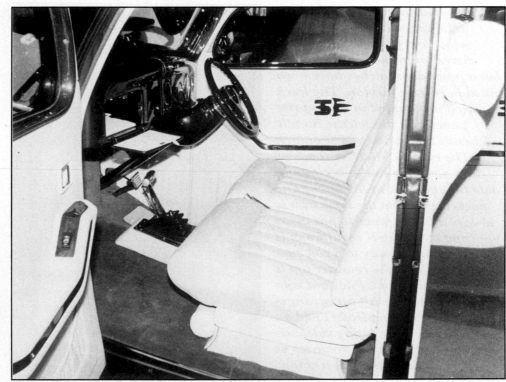

designed and executed the interior of their particular street rods. It's the same old story. It isn't necessary to copy someone else's ideas to the letter, just incorporate aspects of several others into the general styling of your own car and all of a sudden you have your own new concept! But don't forget the basic rules, what you incorporate into your

No, you're not looking at the interior of a late model car. This is in fact the interior of a fiberglass bodied repro '34 Ford coupe that incorporates many late model components including the entire dash from an Australian Holden sedan. Owner Graeme Bevis used everything he could from the Holden including console and fittings, steering column, demister vents and seats.

Simple clean design looks outstanding in this Model A Ford roadster. Retaining the stock instrument bezel maintains the authenticity of the Model A but new gauges have been incorporated into the bezel along with contemporary style warning lights. Matching milled aluminum pedal pads look tidy and the fact that the pedals match each other perfectly helps to make the whole interior look simple and efficient. Nicely trimmed carpet edges and a protective heel mat add the finishing touches.

own car still needs to suit the style of the car you are building. No good going with an ultra modern tweed fabric moulded style interior trim job if you are building a nostalgia car. Likewise a polished aluminium competition style interior would look way out of place in a resto-rod.

Let's spend some time checking how other rodders have tackled the styling of their street rod interiors.

The ultra-integrated look is executed to perfection in this '37 Ford with the same fabric trim used to cover everything except the dash. A simple dash layout with readily available accessory gauges looks more sophisticated thanks to a smoked plexiglass insert. Blending the steering column mount into the lower part of the dash gives the appearance of more interior space and a tilt column makes driving totally comfortable.

Just because you own an early street rod doesn't mean you can't enjoy the comforts of modern motoring. In this '37 Ford a late model tilt steering column has been incorporated along with a lower dash extension that incorporates outlets for an air conditioning system. Once again we find a piece of smoked plexiglass being used to provide an integrated appearance for the dash.

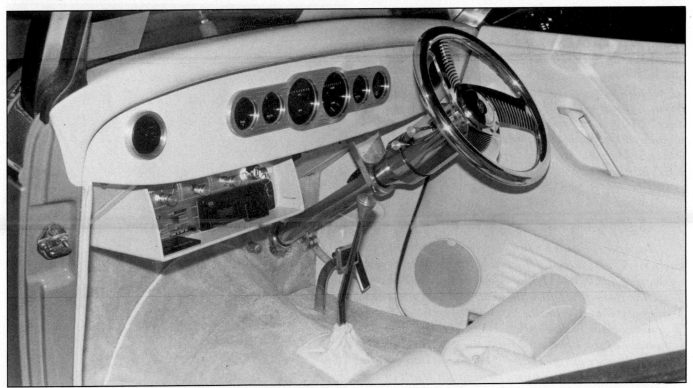

Russell Wright shows us how to design an interior that utilises many common aftermarket components to finish up with a theme that suits the style of car. Milled and polished aluminum and stainless steel combines with the sanitary appearance of white leather for a clinically clean interior. Drop down compartment houses and conceals the sound system, accessory switches and air conditioning controls. Russell's phantom '34 Ford Victoria phaeton is a regular show winner in Australia.

Another example of a late model dash being successfully incorporated into an early body. This example is a Nissan Skyline dash that has been narrowed and fitted into Barry Cook's '35 Ford coupe. The aftermarket woodgrained steering wheel picks up on the same theme used on the Nissan gauge cluster for an integrated appearance. Using a late model steering column usually means you get stalk controls for lights, wipers, etc. which overcomes the need to incorporate them into your dash.

Incorporating late model components into an early street rod doesn't have to be a complex operation. Look how the late model steering column has been fitted into this '35 Ford without disturbing the essentially stock dash panel. Simple covers have been made to tie the column to the bottom of the dash and hide the column mount.

Accessory gauges have been used in a simple layout with the main units straight in front of the driver for easy monitoring. A fire extinguisher mounted in a convenient location in the passenger compartment is advisable in all cars.

If you use a late model collapsible type steering column in your street rod why not take the time to also incorporate the slide mounts that will allow it to still collapse in the event of an accident, as it was originally designed to do? This '37 Ford sedan uses a plain design to locate accessory gauges in the original dash and the sound system is hidden inside the glove compartment.

Manuel Cambourakis' '28 Model A roadster is a strong street/strip performer and it has an interior to suit. Large competition style gauges are mounted in a dash that combines elements of the original Model A dash and a later '32 Ford unit.

There's no reason why the rear seat passengers shouldn't enjoy the same comfort as the front seat passengers. Ian Dawson incorporated bucket seats in the rear of his '34 Ford sedan and all four seats feature a special embroidered flying eagle motif that adds an individual touch to the whole interior. Note the battery isolation switch mounted in the rear seat base, a good idea in any rod for quick access to the power source in the case of an emergency.

This shot of Tony Kuchel's '37 Ford shows how he used the area under each front seat for storage and to locate the battery. The steel seat base mounts pivot back for access to the storage bins but have secure latches to hold them firmly in place during normal use. There's a fire extinguisher close at hand in front of the driver's seat base too.

Tom Farrugia uses his show display to give us an inside look at his clever storage compartment under the seat of his T bucket. Tools live under there too and important safety items such as a fire extinguisher and battery isolation switch fall readily to hand. Note how the parking brake handle has been recessed into the seat base to save valuable floor space.

Adjustable modular style late model seats covered in black leather provide the basis for the entire design of this '37 Ford coupe interior that also uses milled aluminum extensively but then makes it look different by painting or anodising it all black. Once again a neat steering column cover is used to tidy up the under dash area. Owners are Terry and Debbie Young of Rockford, Illinois.

Always think safety when building your street rod and include safety equipment inside the car wherever you can. Here a Model A sedan has been equipped with retractable lap-sash seat belts. Extra steel reinforcing is required behind the trim panels either side of the rear window to provide secure upper mounts. Design them into your own street rod right from the start.

Tony Kuchel has incorporated many late model car type features in his '37 Ford coupe. Just one of them is the forward folding rear seat backs that gives access to the trunk from inside or outside the vehicle. That large roll across the top of the seats also has a purpose, it hides accessory tail lights hidden in the lower section of the rear windows.

Clever integrated design of this '32 Ford roadster is a big feature. You don't sit in this car, you wear it! Note how the speaker grilles, inside door release and interior lights have all been blended into the trim rather than added as an afterthought.

Plenty of simple changes here that could easily be accomplished by the home based rod builder. Note the simple gauge layout in a polished dash panel, clean and simple tilt steering column mount and drink holders incorporated into the centre console. The seat bases also look tidy with covers to hide the adjusting mechanism. Another clever idea is the protective heel mat sewn into the carpet that also extends partly up the transmission tunnel.

Here's another way to incorporate bucket seats into an early roadster. The door trim theme is continued through to the rumble seat area leaving the bucket seats to "float" in the cabin space. Also note where the speakers have been located behind the trim but as close to the passenger's ear as possible, an important consideration in a topless roadster if you want to hear the music while blasting down the highway.

Neil Baker's fiberglass bodied '33 Ford roadster has a street competition style throughout, including the interior. Apart from the competition look of the interior, the roll bar and full harness seat belts will provide extra protection for the occupants.

Even a roadster pickup can have retractable lap-sash seat belts. Look closely and you can see how they have been incorporated into this phantom '34 Ford roadster pickup with the upper mount in the forward corner of the quarter panel.

Below: More clever storage space is revealed under the seat of this Willys roadster. It holds tools and a first aid kit. The lower door jamb area also provides a handy mounting point for a battery isolation switch. Chrome trim and vinyl is used to provide a tidy, finished appearance to the floor and console area.

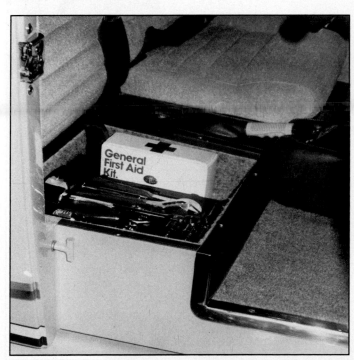

Above: Accessory gauges are used well in this '34 Chevy sedan where they have been carefully positioned so they are easily visible through the steering wheel. Simple switches mounted in the center of the dash are perfectly in keeping with the overall simple styling of this tidy interior.

Street rod interiors don't come much better appointed than Ron Smit's '39 Chevy sedan. The latest, state of the art digital gauges are used in the dash along with a milled billet aluminum steering wheel. Many other milled aluminum parts have been custom made for this interior including the demister outlets on top of the dash. The lower half of the dash has been extended to give additional space to accommodate the air conditioning system. The overall shot of the interior below shows how the console has been extended all the way through to the rear seats so that the passengers back there can enjoy the ducted air conditioning too. They also have a TV to watch that is mounted in the rear end of the console. The whole interior is luxuriously appointed and incorporates all the features of a top of the line late model luxury car.

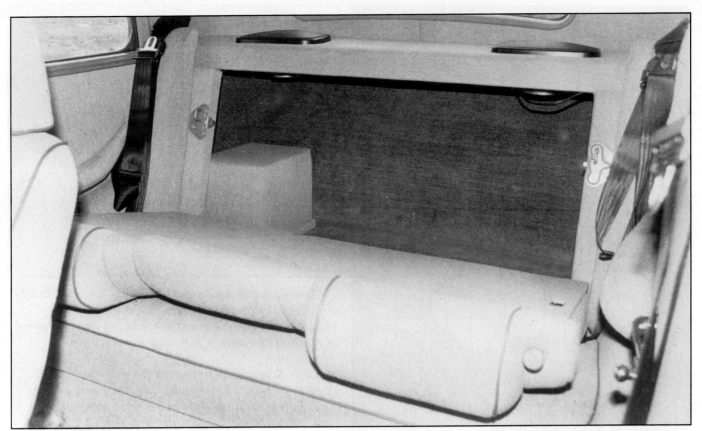

Many early sedans don't have a trunk that is accessible from outside the vehicle. In these type of rods a late model seat with pivoting backrests can often be adapted to suit and it makes access to the trunk space easy while still maintaining a classy looking interior. As you can see in Ian Ward's '34 Ford tudor it also means access to the shelf mounted speakers is easy and the battery is hidden in here too! Often the rear seat can be moved forward a little from its standard location giving more trunk space.

Here's the dash of another right hand drive '39 Chevy sedan. Again an extra panel has been added to the lower edge of the dash to provide mounting space for the air conditioning and sound system. Note how the steering column has also been neatly built into this lower panel for a fully integrated look. The balance of the dash remains essentially stock but late model gauges behind a smoked plexiglass panel and billet aluminum demister outlets hint that this car has been updated for safer, more comfortable operation.

Above: A cut and shut '37 Ford dash looks like an original fitting in Chris Edgecombe's '30 Model A roadster. Accessory gauges are clustered in front of the driver for easy observation.

Left: Stylised sports seats from a late model Ford look right at home in this '34 Ford coupe. Note how neat the seat base covers are and how well the carpet is fitted and finished.

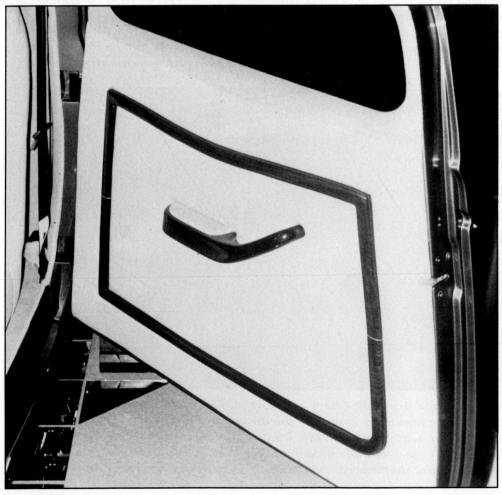

This '33 Ford three window coupe has an interesting trim style displayed here in its door panel. The fabric trim is highlighted with a wooden insert that has been polished and laquered to perfection. The wood is Western Australian Jarrah which is a beautiful deep, rich, red colour when treated this way. The coupe is owned by Brenton Dalwood.

Early fenders don't come any smoother than those on this Model A coupe. The front fender, running board and valance panels are all joined together to form one panel and painted to match the lower half of the body. Not a single mounting bolt is visible anywhere and the headlight bar has been eliminated too. To carry the theme through completely the fender welting has been left out to enhance the simple, clean approach of the whole car.

Probably the most popular comment you will hear from older passing admirers of your street rod will be directed at your running boards. They will reminisce for hours over the car they or their parents used to have that sported those fabulous running boards. There's no doubt they are an important part of the styling of any early car. It's just a bonus that they are also very practical for getting in and out of the car! Once more the treatment you give them on your particular project will have a tremendous bearing on how your finished rod looks.

These days it is very common for street rods to feature plain painted versions of these running boards. There's a twofold reason for this. Sure in most cases it just plain looks good (but not always – remember what I said earlier about keeping the style of your car in context from one end to the other?). Painted running boards do generally look best if they are very smooth and plain in design. Of course that means you can probably make them

up yourself, saving the cost of repro original style boards or the cost of resurrecting a set of damaged originals, if you can find them in the first place. The down side is that now you have to go to great pains to protect the nice painted finish. That can be far more trouble than it's worth, especially since the great masses don't generally understand that a painted running board is no longer for running on!

Retaining the original style running board doesn't necessarily mean you can't still make your own, but you may need to be a little more clever to duplicate the original styling without having to shell out for a set of new repro items. Obviously if you are rodding one of the more obscure or less popular makes of early cars repros won't be available anyway. You can still refine the original design so the running board doesn't look out of place but does in fact enhance the overall styling of the car. It all goes back to keeping the car in context from one end to the other.

Here's another good example of the clean, painted approach to running boards on an early Model A Ford tourer that has been converted to two door configuration. In this instance the fenders, running boards and valance panels remain as separate items but they fit together very neatly with no fender welting in between. The end result is a clean integrated look with no "uglies" to distract attention from the overall clean lines of the car.

The same principle applies to the fenders. Some early thirties cars had elaborate fender designs that suit the overall style of the car in original or restored form but can look a little ungainly on a rodded version. This is one area where some nineties street rodders are getting really clever, changing or refining the design just enough to the point where it looks far better than the original, yet to the untrained eye the alteration is hard to pick. There are several examples of such "tricks" in this chapter.

Many early fenders were quite narrow being

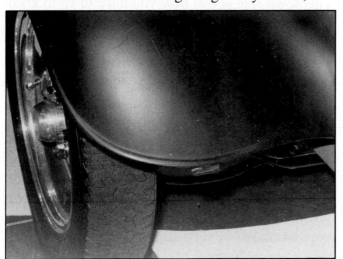 

Finding a place to mount turn signals is a never-ending saga for the street rodder. The problem becomes even more acute if you don't run bumpers. Here's one answer shown from inside and out. Small brackets have been moulded into the inside leading edge of the fiberglass fender to provide an attaching point for small accessory turn signals. Only the lens of the signal is exposed when viewed from the front of the car.

The painted running board style lends itself well to non-Ford street rods too. In this case a mid-thirties Dodge coupe has perfect fitting running boards painted to match the body. Folding up new running boards and giving them this treatment is often a practical way to overcome the lack of, or the poor condition of, original items.

only designed to accommodate a three or four inch wide tire and they don't come close to covering the 10 inch monsters you want to run on the back of your street rod. Often the answer is as simple as widening the fender to suit, but care needs to be excercised to make sure the widened fender doesn't look ungainly. An option we are seeing chosen more and more is to move the inner fender area inwards to provide more tire clearance. Sometimes even a combination of the two cures is necessary to keep the overall style of the car in context. There's that phrase again!

There's one more trick you should be aware of in this fender and running board area that works well on almost any car. In their original form most early cars used fender welting at all the joints between body and fender, valance panel and fender, or fender and running board. In many cases the car in street rod form looks much better if this fender welting is left out and the panels just bolted firmly together. With today's modern roads and the extra strength built into a street rod chassis, eliminating much of the flexing, the welting often isn't necessary anyway. You will have to ensure that all the panels fit together very well to achieve the best result but this is a fairly common "omission" that usually works well and can often be the only

If you can't find a way to fit turn signals in an unobtrusive way why not make them a feature of the car as has been done on this '27 Model T Ford? Lenses that suit the curvature of the fender lip have been flush fitted into the fender with access to the housing gained from underneath.

109

If you like the painted running board style but want to avoid having them scratched as much as possible you will like this neat idea. The running boards have been painted but then rubber side protection strips have been used to keep shoes from coming into contact with the painted surface. Simple and very effective.

Here's another version of the painted running board with protection strips to stop shoes scratching the surface. This time aluminum strips have been used on a '36 Ford running board. Adding a magnetic "no-step" sign when parked is added insurance.

Widened rear fenders have been used on Bruce Newbold's Model A Ford tudor and they have been linked at the rear with a non-standard apron that also acts as a housing for the tail lights. Look closely at the edge of the fender and you will also see neat turn signals mounted with the fender brace bolt leaving only the lens of the signal exposed. Running boards have also been widened at the rear.

reason one street rod will look much better than a similar car right alongside. You might not readily see the difference but you will notice that one car looks better balanced than the other without necessarily realising why. The next best alternative if you want to retain the welting, or can't get the panels to align quite as well as you would like, is to colour code the welting so that it "disappears" into the panels.

Step aboard as we take you on a pictorial running board and fender tour.

Another Model A Ford running board displays a couple of different innovations. The running board has been painted to match the rest of the body but this time the owner has added a raised reveal to the top surface and laid protection strips inside that reveal. Also notice how body welting has been used but it too is body color so it almost becomes invisible to the casual viewer.

Russell Wright's phantom '34 Ford Victoria phaeton has painted running boards and fenders that are so smooth you can barely pick the mating joins. The lack of fender welting once again highlights how good the fit of all the panels is and the use of recessed tail lights means the graceful sweep of the '34 fenders is uninterrupted from front to rear.

The painted running board on Barry Cook's '35 Ford coupe gives the car an integrated appearance because the color of the lower half flows from one end to the other without interruption.

Despite all the trick running boards we see on modern street rods sometimes it's just as effective to leave the standard item in place. Peter Laxton's '39 Ford coupe is a perfect example of just how good the original rubber covered running board can be when it is fitted to perfection as is the case here. Combined with bright red paint and clean, black tires this is a classic combination that will always look attractive

In stark contrast to the stock running boards shown above are these completely custom built items fitted to Mike Fitzpatrick's '39 Chevy sedan. These are made from sheet steel and have the Chevy Bowtie emblem pressed into their surfaces. Finally the running boards have been painted to match the body which means "no stepping allowed."

Once upon a time the factories supplied you with a new car that was just that – a car and not much else. If you wanted extra features they usually came from the aftermarket in the form of accessories. Buy a new car today and there won't be much in the way of practical accessories that you can add on because they are built into the car in an endeavour to swing you to that particular brand. The discerning street rodder has to some extent grown a little soft as a result and likes to incorporate many accessories into his early car even though it was notoriginally designed to have them. Such things as air conditioning, elaborate sound systems, turning indicators and seat belts fall into this category. The problem faced by the street rodder is to incorporate these extras into the car in a friendly manner. You don't want them to look like an afterthought.

This is one area where the rapidly expanding aftermarket that has flourished around the street rod hobby has helped a lot. Take air conditioning as just one example. There is now a large range of systems and components to choose from in this area and they are increasingly being designed to complement early body designs. Units are becoming more and more compact in design to suit the restricted under dash space in most street rods and the visible components are usually designed in such a way as to suit fitting to early dashboards.

Radio antennae is another area where designs have been developed to be as inconspicuous as possible or even to remain out of sight altogether. If you do wish to fit an external antenna make sure you position and fix it in such a way as to be as unobtrusive as possible. Some brands are even able to be removed from their mount which makes it easy to ensure your parked street rod looks its best. Using this type of antenna also minimises the chances of it being damaged or causing damage to your street rod when you are not around. The ultimate antenna for your street rod could be one of the new remote mount style that have recently come onto the market. These can be mounted inside the car. Using one of these means you don't

Mounting a CB/radio antenna can be a real pain for street rodders. It needs to be somewhere exposed to operate properly but you don't want it spoiling the neat lines of your vehicle. Here's one solution where the antenna has been mounted on a simple bracket that attaches to the tail light bracket using the original tail light mounting bolts. Look closely and you will see that the underside of the tail light staunchion has been filled to hide the wiring and then chrome plated for a neat, solid appearance.

have to remember to remove it either.

These are just a couple of examples of accessory items that might find a place in your street rod. No doubt there are many others and we're sure you will find some exciting ideas amongst the photographic collection included here.

Right: This radio antenna is small enough and flexible enough that it won't be damaged by accidental contact and mounted at the rear of this Anglia it looks perfectly at home. To further help it blend into the surrounds it is painted body color.

Another radio antenna, this time you have to look hard to see it mounted via small chrome plated brackets to the door pillar of this Model A Ford tudor. It is even harder to pick because the mounts align with the door hinges.

A simple bracket that mounts in the stake bed hole of Ken Baker's Model A pickup keeps this CB radio antenna out of the way or it can be easily and quickly removed altogether if necessary.

Finding a convenient place to mount the radio antenna has been solved by the owner of this Australian '34 Chevy sedan by using a late model General Motors antenna from a Holden Commodore. It has its own recessed mounting plate that is easily recessed into any curved panel such as the top of the cowl as shown here. The antenna can be fully retracted into this mount.

Another clever use of a late model radio antenna on an early body, this time a '27 Ford T roadster. This type of antenna is usually found on the windshield pillar of small imported cars but is easily transferred to the cowl and windshield post of the T. Note also the oval shaped turn signal mounted on the side of the cowl. This is another donor item from a small imported car that really suits street rod styling. In fact they are often used in conjunction with the old favorite '39 Ford teardrop tail lights used by street rodders.

Not only are the custom windshield posts on this Deuce roadster really slick but check out the very neat rear view mirrors mounted inside the posts near the base. Mounted here they don't protrude from the vehicle but are still easily accessible to the driver. With a roof fitted the mirrors could possibly be less effective but look closely and you will see that they could be rotated outwards to extend beyond the outer edge of the windshield post and consequently gain a wider viewing angle.

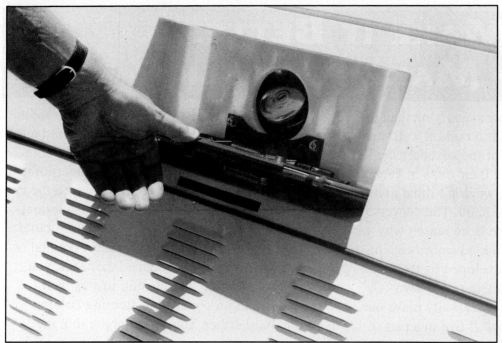

A recessed plate always looks good on the back of a street rod like this '34 Chevy roadster but if you use a pivoting plate mount like this one you can also use it to hide the fuel filler cap. Note the third eye brake light mounted in the lower body panel under the plate recess as well. Louvers tell you this is a hot rod.

Gunter Maric's '35 Ford phaeton has a superb one-piece lift-off roof that really suits the overall style of the car. On closer inspection there appears to be no visible means of retaining the top. The photo at right reveals the secret. Access to the retaining bolt is gained through a hole hidden in the door jamb.

MAKE IT BETTER - MAKE IT SAFER

Few aspects of life are more satisfying than to build your own street rod and to build it well. It is well documented that many of the advances in automotive technology found their roots in the hot rodding sphere. That's okay, we don't mind giving the auto manufacturers a free hand. The converse is also true however and there is no reason why we shouldn't take advantage of the advancements in technology that have been developed by the major manufacturers. We can turn them to our own advantage in our street rods and usually make our cars better and safer as a result. I live in a part of the world that has led the way, to quite an extent, when it comes to the incorporation of safety items into cars and the road system. The result is a dramatically reduced road toll and none of us can realistically argue against that outcome. I am talking here of such things as the compulsory use of seat belts, collapsible steering columns, dual circuit brakes, etc..

Of course it isn't always easy or even possible to incorporate all modern safety systems into an early car that wasn't designed to accept them in the first place. However many can be incorporated if you plan early enough to build them into the car. These days there is no excuse for not using dual circuit brakes for instance. If you expect to build a car that can provide road performance to equal or better that from factory produced cars then you obviously need to be able to stop just as well.

Incorporating a collapsible steering column isn't that hard either. You might argue that the dash bracket and associated retaining mechanism that is designed to slide free in the event of an accident doesn't look very attractive, but you won't be too concerned about appearances if you are catapulted towards your steering column at sixty miles an hour in an accident. Besides you are a hot rodder, right, so remanufacturing that mount to look better, but still incorporate its collapsing

The original Model A Ford fuel tank in the author's pickup has been gutted to provide space for the electrical fuse block and control panel where it will be out of sight but easily accessible. This area also provides a place for the windshield washer system which is filled through the original cowl mounted fuel filler cap. Note that one of the original fuel tank baffles has been left in place to provide strength and rigidity for the steering column mount. Large holes in the back of the tank and the baffle are for wiring to pass through. The large opening in the bottom of the tank also allows access to the rear of the gauge panel without having to remove it.

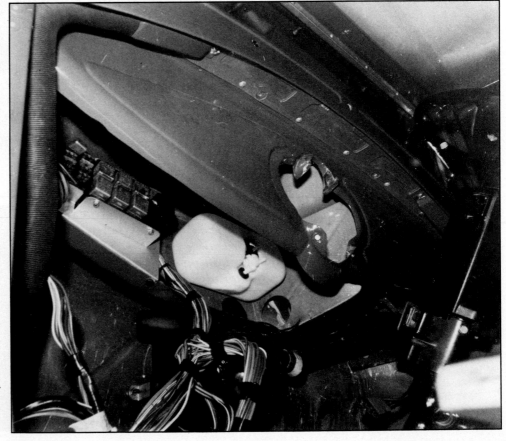

Here's a good example of how a demister system can be fitted into an early street rod. The original ventilation "box" under the windshield has been sealed off with aluminum sheet and demister outlet fittings made to feed into this section. With the original dash rail in place all of this system is hidden from view. The picture at right shows how the lower windshield frame rail has been drilled to provide demister outlets.

ability is just one more small challenge to overcome. While you're at it why not incorporate a modern breakaway style rear view mirror? Look hard enough and you will even find versions in some small cars that also incorporate a tidy interior light.

Same goes for a dual circuit braking system. You may have to be a little more clever in designing the mount and providing the space for the booster and its associated vacuum line but that's easily done if you plan it into the process right from the start. It's a good idea to include an adjustable brake proportioning valve into the system too so you can fine tune the braking for best performance.

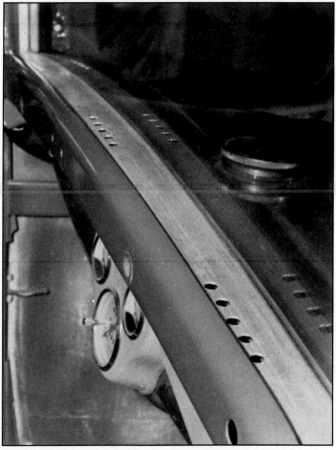

Here's a simple but decorative way to add a safety stop to a suicide front end in a T bucket. The chrome plated and sculptured cover on the spring mounting pad has been shaped so that in the event of a shackle or spring failure the cover "catches" the axle on the way down and prevents the chassis from coming into contact with the pavement.

Most registration authorities require that all vehicles have red reflectors at the rear so that the vehicle is visible when parked at night with the lights off. Fitting such reflectors is often aesthetically undesirable on an early car but the problem can be overcome. In this instance Michael Smart has used a section of a late model brake light lens that incorporates a reflector and cut it to shape so that it fits his Model A tail light. Now the reflector is in the original tail light!

Wet weather vision is another area where some street rods are not up to an acceptable modern standard. Fitting a simple single speed wiper may satisfy the legal requirement in your state but you will never regret using more modern, two speed multi-blade systems if you can find a way to incorporate them. The first time you are caught in a sudden storm on the open road you will thank yourself for making the effort to use modern wipers. What's more most of them include an auto-park feature when you switch them off. Take it one step further and wire your low beam headlights to come on at the same time and you will be right up to date with the latest regulations for some states.

Return to the interior of the car and we can find a couple of other areas where modern refinements can find a home in your street rod as well. The inclusion of demisters is required in some parts of the world and while that might seem impossible in some early cars there usually is a way it can be done. We don't think twice about chopping a top or modifying a fender or other major item on our street rod yet ask us to incorporate some of these modern safety items and we will often find an excuse for not doing so. Like I said before, these things should just be another hurdle to overcome in our quest for the best street rod we can possibly build. That doesn't necessarily equate to most expensive either, but it could equate to most clever!

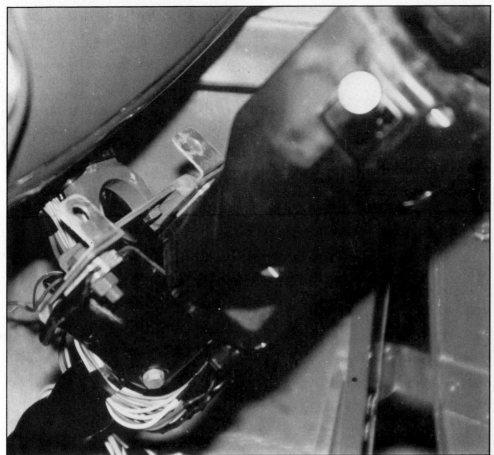

The original Model A Ford steering column mount remains in place in this rod but a new mounting bracket has been made to bolt to this original bracket and provide new mounting positions for the late model Toyota column being used. Note how the collapsable slides have been retained to mount the column so that in the event of an accident the column will still collapse as it is designed to do. Light aluminum right angled brackets are made to accept a cover to hide all this from view (see next photo).

The decorative cover panel that hides the mounting brackets shown above is made from an aluminum baking dish. It's simple but it works and looks like it belongs here. The simple plastic toggle switches operate engine and heater fans and perform double duty as they are all that holds this cover in place via the simple aluminum right angle brackets shown in the previous photo. In the event of an accident the column will collapse through this cover plate and if it happens to catch the edge of the cover the plastic switches would break away and let the very light aluminum cover deform accordingly. Study late model vehicles to see how they achieve the same results for ideas for your own street rod.

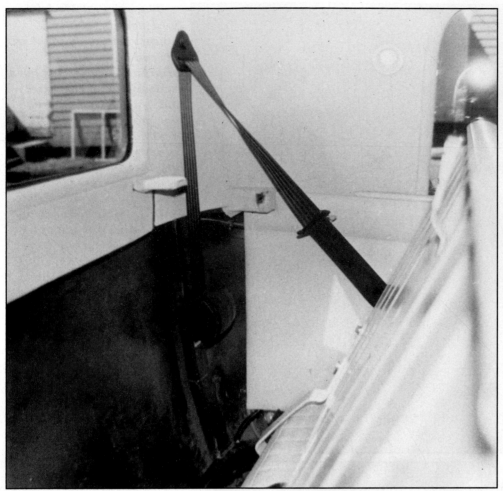

Retractable lap/sash seat belts are a great safety addition to any street rod and in fact are a required item in some jurisdictions. Take the time to fit them while you're building your next project. Here we see a retractable belt fitted in the rear of a Model A Ford tudor. Note the substantial steel member that has been added behind the seat and integrated into the body substructure to provide secure mounting points for the belt. A "bump stop" has been added to prevent the seat from moving past a certain point, leaving the belt free to move in and out of its reel without restriction.

This time we have a retractable lap/sash belt fitted into the front of a '32 Ford tudor. The upper mount is through the door pillar which should be reinforced to provide a secure mounting point. If using an original steel body you can usually insert a section of rectangular steel tube to reinforce the pillar but if using a fiberglass body you may need to replace wood body reinforcing with steel to provide this upper mount. Don't mount seat belts through wooden body framing without substantial steel reinforcing.

Mounting retractable lap/sash seat belts in a roadster is a little more difficult, but not impossible. Using a roll bar as the upper mount is one way to overcame the lack of upper body mounting points. This example has been cleverly designed to incorporate an opening in the seat trim to allow the belt to slide through and the reel can be mounted at the base of the roll bar out of sight.

One of the simplest safety items you can add to your street rod is a battery isolation switch. The author incorporated this one in the seat riser of his Model A pickup where it is out of the way in normal operation but easily accessible if necessary. The battery is mounted under the floor in close proximity which is also a good idea as it keeps voltage drop along the cables to a minimum. Note the use of rubber grommets where the cables pass throught the steel floor.

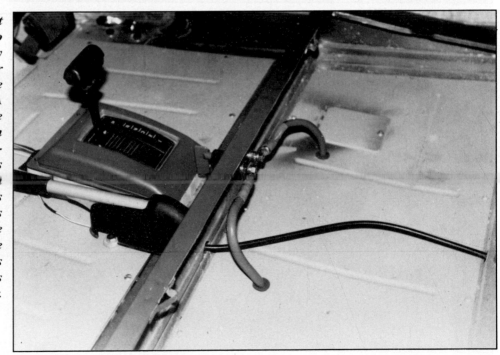

One of the best safety devices you can fit in a street rod is a fire extinguisher. The best place to mount one is on the floor somewhere within reach of the driver as has been done in this '38 Ford coupe. By mounting the extinguisher here the driver can get to it even if he happens to be trapped in the car in the event of an accident that results in a fire. Make sure you fit one in your street rod.

Below: If at all possible try to fit retractable seat belts in your street rod. However in doing so make sure you incorporate mounts that are strong enough to do the job. In a case like this where the mount is in the roof substructure you may need to add steel reinforcing that connects to the door pillar. Don't mount them through wooden substructures.

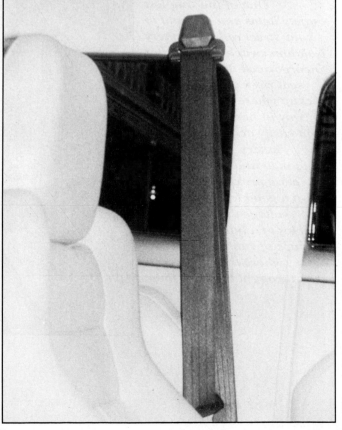

An electrical fault can spell disaster in a street rod so it is always a good idea to incorporate a battery isolater switch. It is much quicker to flick the isolater switch to off than try to remove a battery terminal in a hurry.

124

Fitting late model burst proof door latches has more than one benefit. Not only are they safer than an original style latch in the event of an accident but they also hold the door in such a way that it doesn't bounce in its opening. However it isn't always possible to fit burst proof latches in all early doors but you can still incorporate the anti-bounce feature by making your own pin and locater as shown here in conjunction with the original latch. The pin is simply screwed to the door and the locater is screwed to the door pillar. The locater is simply two pieces of steel plate that sandwich a piece of teflon with the center cut out to allow for the head of the pin to locate firmly within it as the door closes.

Clear vision in wet weather is very desirable for your street rod. This triple wiper set up mounted in the header panel of a Model A Ford tudor is a proven swap. The wiper system comes from a four wheel drive Nissan Patrol and three of them cleans almost the entire glass area. What's more they are dual speed with automatic park and the arms are shaped so that the blades park horizontally across the top of the windshield.

Retractable seat belts can be fitted in your street rod in a tidy manner as shown here. This example uses the rear seat retractable belts from a late model vehicle where the upper mount sits flat on the parcel shelf. Make sure the shelf is properly reinforced so that the mounting point is at least equivalent in strength to that in the late model vehicle.

Competition styled street rods look tough but they have to be practical too. Remember that on the street you will be driving such a car without all the protective gear that a racing driver wears so you need to make some compromises. That's why the rollcage in this Anglia street rod has been heavily padded in the vicinity of the passengers heads.

How do you get a Model T tudor to sit this low to the ground? Look carefully and you will pick up a few clues. For instance, note the depth of the valance panels and the way they fit to the fender at the front. Now check out the depth of the engine hood side panels. A little shorter than usual? Clever engineering on this car has resulted in a really trick street rod. The chassis has been stepped up at front and rear to allow the ride height to be really low yet still retain full suspension travel and a stock body, at least externally. Reshaping the valance panel hides it all from all but the most observant viewer.

Some aspects of building street rods are very satisfying. In particular those special items that set your rod apart from the rest. For the street rodder, finding a way to overcome a problem, making something fit where it normally wouldn't, or just incorporating some extra safety or convenience device that others said couldn't be done is always a buzz. There's a real sense of achievement in finding solutions to problems that help to make your finished rod special, if not in the eyes of everybody else at least in your own eyes.

How often have you checked out the latest rods at recent events and come across something really clever that another rodder has incorporated into his or her street rod that causes you to stop in your tracks and exclaim; "Now why didn't I think of that?"

This chapter is about all those situations. Here's a package of just plain good ideas that you could incorporate into your own street rod or modify to make yet another clever idea. Some are so simple they seem obvious, especially after you see them used. Others are so subtle that you may not even notice what has been done until someone points it out to you. Still others are quite complex and in some instances not for the inexperienced to tackle, but the end result is often well worth the effort, resulting in a street rod that is truly unique.

Repairing original stainless steel or diecast body trim can be expensive but here's a clever way to overcome the problem. All the original trim has been retained on this '40 Ford sedan but it has all been painted to match the body paint color. This way the original trim can be repaired and filled as necessary and since it won't be polished or plated again the paint hides any repairs that have been made. At the same time the car appears more high-tech than is really the case as the all-paint look is popular. Even the running boards have received the all-paint look, including the flames! The end result is a street rod that is right up there with the current trends but hasn't been expensive to build.

Years of experience has resulted in street rods that are often so refined they can truly compare with the latest expensive factory produced super cars. Others are really simple, low-dollar concepts that cost almost nothing to incorporate, but result in a street rod that turns heads just because of their simplicity.

Come on, let's go exploring the world of just plain good ideas. Street rodding is fun!

Some common aftermarket wheels feature only a simple plastic centre cap and often they don't blend in with the overall style of the car. This owner has machined up an alloy cap to give his wheels a totally integrated appearance.

Model A tudors aren't particularly strong in the roof area so filling the roof with a steel insert helps considerably. Using a ribbed insert from a donor late model station wagon adds style to an otherwise large blank space and helps prevent drumming from the flat panel. Take a look at the sun visor on this car as well. It has been louvered in reverse to let the air pass through. Without the louvers a Model A sun visor is like a built-in head wind and after many miles the constant buffetting can actually damage the mounts from the constant flexing. Finally, check out the novel mounting point for the billet aluminum rear view mirror. By mounting it to the underside of the window opening it doesn't look like just another add-on item.

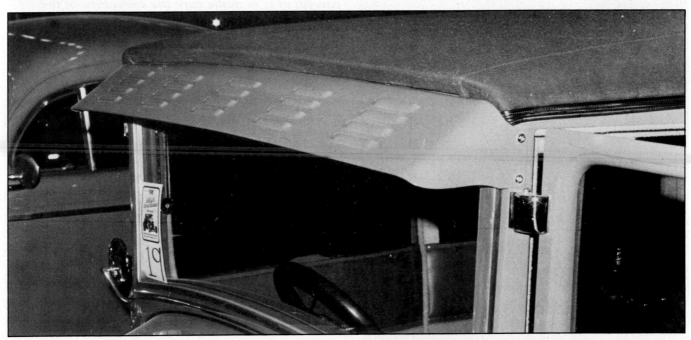

Here's another version of the louvered Model A Ford visor. In this case the vinyl roof covering extends all the way to the front. In the standard form the vinyl stops just short of the front and has a painted steel panel at the leading edge. Extending the vinyl all the way forward overcomes the need to find an original front edge panel (they are often rusty) and it also makes the roof more weatherproof.

Careful searching of the wrecking yard will reveal a ribbed roof insert from a wagon or delivery van that can be used to fill and strengthen the roof of early Ford based street rods such as this '34 Ford sedan. The main thing to be careful of is to make sure the curvature of the donor roof matches that of your street rod and that you don't have to shorten the ribs. Ian Dawson used a Mazda van roof in this example.

The flip out fuel filler door in the custom made pickup bed of this '34 Ford pickup is a neat addition but also take a look at the tail light. It is mounted using a simple home made aluminum bracket and stainless steel flex tube has been used to cover the wiring as on headlights. It is all very simple but very neat. A rubber grommet finished off the installation where the flex tube passes through the side of the bed.

Normally the wiring enters a Deitz headlight through the hollow mounting bolt. The author changed his to take a shorter route to the grille shell by drilling a hole low on the back of the light. Rubber grommets and flex tubing tidy up the installation which now looks more like a factory installation.

With the headlight insert removed you can see another neat trick here. The turn signal has been mounted below the headlight on its own simple mounting bracket and a small hole drilled in the bottom of the headlight bucket to allow the turn signal wire to pass straight up into the headlight. Here it is combined with the headlight wires and routed to the grille shell through the flex tubing.

Left: Extra protection for the paintwork on either side of this Model A rumble seat is afforded by the cover panels that match the interior trim. Just flip them inside before closing the lid and nobody even knows they are there.

Need somewhere to hide all the wiring components in your Model A Ford? Kevin Kendall added a false firewall to his tudor and then used the space in between to hide the wiring control panel and associated hardware. Removable, clip-in cover panels provide easy access for maintenance. Heater hoses and the speedo cable share the space with the wiring.

Recessed license plates always look tidy but finding a place for the light can be a problem. In this case holes have been drilled in the underside of the top of the recess and lights mounted inside the body. The light shines through but from a normal viewing position all you see is the license plate.

Here's another variation on the license plate illumination requirement. This time the plate has been recessed more at the bottom than the top. An aluminum backing plate not only supports the license plate but has also been folded over at the top to provide a mounting point for the light.

Late model flip out fuel filler doors really help to clean up the lines of any early street rod and this '38 Chevy Utility is no exception. Owner Richard Crooker shows how he hid the release mechanism under the rear fender for easy access when filling. Check out the mounting point for the third eye brake light too.

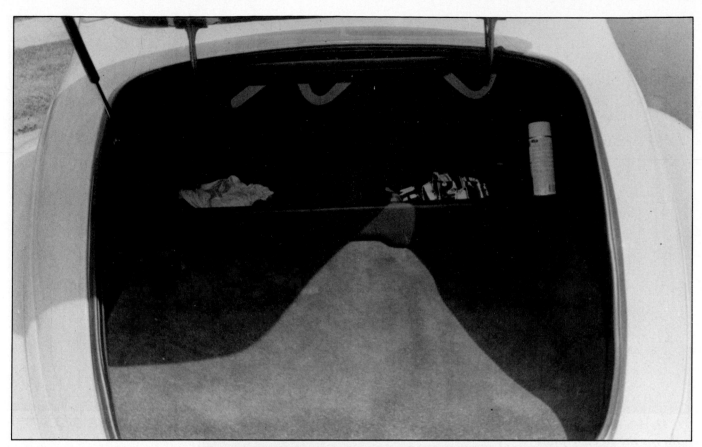

Need a spot to carry all those emergency tools and cleaning equipment for the next rod run? Here's a way to prevent them from sliding around the trunk. A simple container has been made to fit to the shape of the floor at the front of the trunk and a flip up lid keeps everything in place. Covered with vinyl that matches the rest of the trim, it blends right in.

Normally these '39 Ford rear bumper irons would support only the bumper but in this case an extra bar has been added extending from one side to the other and consequently providing a mounting point for the license plate. The bracket is positioned such that when the car is viewed from the rear all you see is the license plate itself dropping down from under the bumper.

Model A pickups didn't have a tonneau cover in original form so there isn't anywhere to attach one. The author overcame the problem on his '30 Model A by making a steel frame that bolts into the stake bed holes in each corner of the bed to support the cover. The tonneau itself is held in position by strips of Velcro material glued to the undersides of the side rails and the front and rear of the new frame. With the whole arrangement removed from the vehicle nothing remains in sight to suggest that a tonneau is ever fitted.

Here's a good example of how careful planning can achieve many things. The front bumper iron on this '37 Ford coupe serves several purposes. It pulls the bumper closer to the body and passes under the fender instead of through it. The bumper iron also acts as a mounting point for the stock stabiliser bar incorporated into a Mitsubishi L300 front end.

Here's a clever storage idea in the rear of a phantom '33 Ford C400 convertible. The rear of the soft top roof zips out to provide access to a lid in the rear parcel shelf that in turn gives access to the area behind the seat from outside the car.

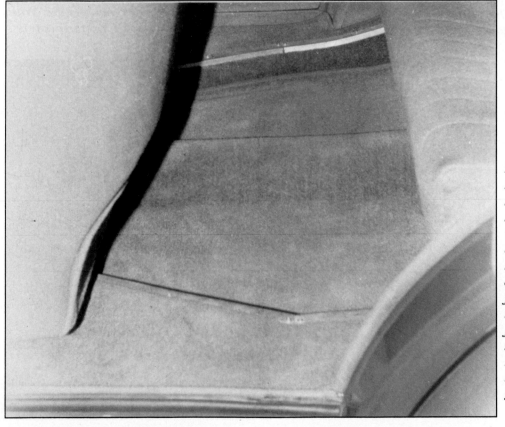

Since the early fifties it has been common to gain more foot room in cars by recessing the floor below the sill levels. No reason why the same approach can't be used in a street rod too. Here is just such an example in the rear floor area of a '34 Chevy tourer. Even though the floor obviously follows the shape of the center X member of the '34 Chassis there is still a considerable gain in foot room.

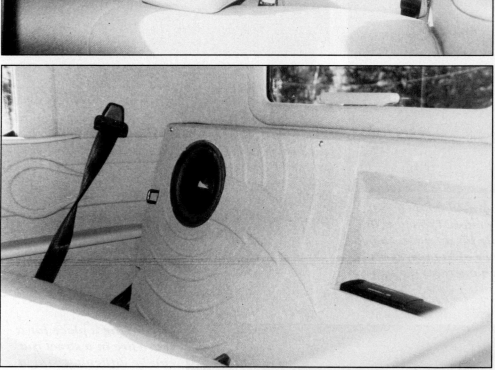

Modern sound systems are nothing short of incredible with their volume control and clarity of sound. However all the equipment associated with gaining that fantastic sound has to go some-where and in a street rod that can be a challenge. Bill Robinson came up with a practical solution in his Model A Ford tudor. The centre armrest folds down in the rear to reveal the basic control panel which is operated by the remote control device shown sitting on the armrest. Fold the whole seat forward and the actual multi-disc CD player is revealed mounted to one side with a speaker on the opposite side. Interior trim has been done in such a way as to highlight the entire installation. Bill can simply load the CD player with his favorite music and head off to the next rod run without ever having to leave his seat to enjoy hours of listening pleasure.

A little thought when trimming your street rod can gain you some extra hidden storage space. The trunk of this '39 Chevy has just such a space right at the rear end with a neat cover that forms part of the normal trunk floor when in the down position. This would be an ideal place to store a few tools and a small jack but still leave the balance of the trunk free for the family's valu-able luggage.

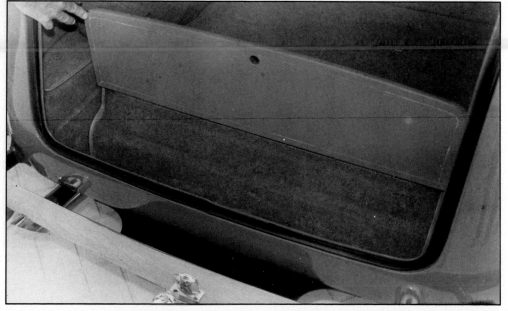

Finding a place to mount turn signals on a T bucket can be difficult but this owner has solved the problem by mounting small accessory lights at the base of the windshield. These small bullet shaped lights are common in auto accessory shops, they're inexpensive and yet they suit the styling of almost any early street rod.

Daniel Cassar has incorporated many trick fittings in his Model A Ford coupe. Typical is this recessed fuel filler with simple lift up door. Note the overflow tube in the corner of the recess and the push button release which operates the trunk latch.

Finding a place for a spare tire in a street rod can be difficult. Using a modern "space saver" spare is often the easiest solution because it will fit in a confined space such as the rumble seat area of this '34 Ford coupe. Most street rods use different tires front and rear so a "space saver" emergency use tire like this is adequate to get you out of trouble until your normal tire can be repaired or replaced.

Take a long look at this one. Model A sedan delivery has been radically restyled in almost every department. The doors have been fitted flush with the body where they normally overlap it and the corners have been radiused to match the window opening. The same has been done to the windshield which now uses no frame and is fitted from inside the body. The cowl has been extensively smoothed and widened slightly so that it blends into the door pillar. The drip rail has been eliminated from above the door and the sunshade blended into and permanently attached to the body. A mountain of very specialised work but with spectacular end results. This is street rod styling at its best.

The seat base is a great place to hide things in a street rod. Robert Riggs used his to locate the trunk and fuel filler door release levers on his '46 Chevy coupe. Both fittings are from late model vehicles but they look right at home in their new location.

The tail light on this '39 Chevy sedan is basically a stock original item but the small turn signal attached to the bottom of it is non-standard. However the two have been matched and combined so that it all appears factory original to the untrained eye.

Flathead Fords always look spectacular when fully dressed in polished finned accessories with painted highlights. Chris Henry has taken the finned thing a step further on his fabulous '27 T roadster pickup by adding a finned aluminum top tank to the radiator. Who makes this period perfect accessory? Would you believe that ribbed tank top is actually from a veteran Daimler and was found at a swap meet!

Here's another clever trick from Chris Henry's T roadster pickup, this time a unique mounting place for the stereo cassette player in the driver's side door pocket. Push it in and it remains out of sight to the casual observer or pull it out and the controls fall readily to hand, even while driving. Note the steering wheel as well. It's a commonly available aftermarket item but the addition of an early V8 emblem in the center gives the whole interior a more traditional style.

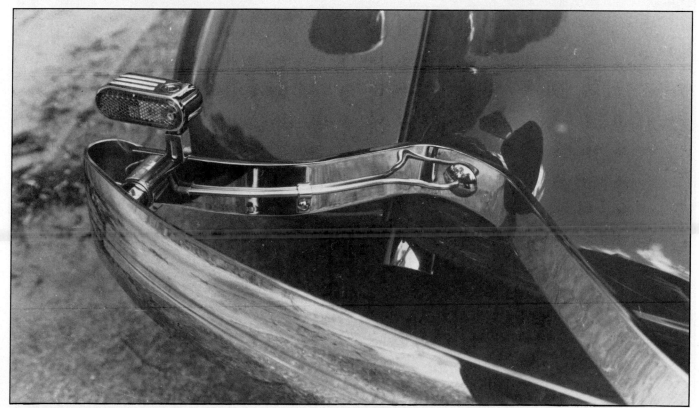

Robert Forbes owns the '34 Ford tudor that this neat piece of detailing work belongs to. The turn signal is custom milled from billet aluminum as is its mounting bracket. The wiring is routed through a polished stainless steel tube that passes down the center of the drilled bumper mounting bolt. It's hard to imagine how such an installation could be made any tidier than this!

Using the glove compartment to house the sound system in a street rod isn't really uncommon but it is still a good idea. There are a couple of other good ideas in Kevin Lewis' '34 Ford tudor. Check out the way the steering column has been mounted so that it retains the original slide locaters that will allow the column to collapse as it was originally intended to in its original vehicle. Also of note is the column mounted gear shift selector that leaves the limited floor space uncluttered.

Finally a perfect example of how attention to detail in the styling of your street rod will pay dividends in the end. Malcolm Case's '32 Ford tudor is perfectly balanced front to rear, inside and out. Even on a dull rainy day this street rod commands attention from street rodders who know what styling street rods is all about.

Larry O'Toole is the publisher of Australian Street Rodding Magazine which he established in 1976. He is also a "hands on hot rodder" who is blessed with the ability to do most of the work on his own street rod projects including bodywork and paint. Raised on a wheat farm at Ultima, Victoria, he moved in 1973 to Castlemaine, a hot bed of hot rodding activity where he now lives with wife, Mary and their four children.

Larry currently has two finished street rods including a Model A tudor that has been on the road for more than 20 years. It is big block Chevy powered and runs on L.P.G. (propane) which is popular as a cheap alternative fuel in southern Australia. His other street rod is a '30 Model A pickup that is Buick V6 powered and has been in active use since 1990. Both cars are almost entirely home-built in Larry's own workshop, the source of many technical articles for Street Rodding Magazine. Other ongoing projects include a '32 Ford hiboy roadster and a '36 Ford flatback tudor.

Previous books on hot rodding compiled and edited by Larry O'Toole and published by Graffiti Publications include the titles; How To Build Your Own Custom Street Car, Street Rodding Gallery, Street Rods In Color, and the Colorful World Of Street Rods.